# *Jacob Fuller*

### Lately of New York

> **Fuller:**
>
> One who fulls cloth; one who shrinks and thickens woolen cloth by moistening, heating, and pressing; one who cleans and finishes cloth

Back cover: Photo by www.tripadvisor.com/LocationPhotos-g48885-Whitehall_New_York.html"><img
alt="Whitehall Photos"

Copywrite © 2011 by K. L. Houk
Printed in the United States of America
First Edition

Disclaimer:

This is a non-profit research document made available to family members and the public for the cost of production. The names are real, the facts are as true as can be found; yet the interpretation of those facts is the work of the compiler. Therefore, those who have additional information, photos, corrections or amendments are urged to forward them for inclusion. This document builds upon the work of Mary Johnston Nussbaum, but is by no means the end of the family stories related. New information is being uncovered daily. The format is such that changes can easily be made and reprinted. Subsequent genealogists may yet unravel the many mysteries and questions raised by this on-going study. They are encouraged to do so!

This book is dedicated to Mary Nussbaum

It is only a small portion of her legacy

2nd Class Petty Officer Mary Johnston, U.S. Navy
Boston, Massachusetts, circa 1945

## Table of Contents

| | | |
|---|---|---|
| Section 1 | Jacob's Story | Page 1 |
| Section 2 | Abel B's Story | Page 26 |
| Section 3 | Jonathan C's Story | Page 37 |
| Section 4 | Sarah E's Story | Page 51 |
| Section 5 | The Missing Link | Page 63 |
| Appendix A | Fullers in Uniform | Page 67 |
| Appendix B | Jacob's Descendents | Page 71 |
| References | | |

# Section 1: JACOB'S STORY

Whitehall, New York, 1812

*"The Fullers were an intensely patriotic family…those whom we know served in the army during the Revolution were Aaron, Sr., …Elijah, Elisha, Ephraim, Gershom, John, Mathew and Samuel….Among a lost list of other Fullers who lived here after the war we find Almon, Abizer, Bartlet, Dayton, Daniel, Jacob, Joseph and Samuel B."* (Holden, 1916-1918)

Southern end of Lake George by fabioj 9/2005

Jacob had mixed feelings as he gazed at Lake George. New artillery had been placed in Fort Edwards and military barracks were under construction west of Church Street. Entrenchments and magazines were being built on the island north of the village. Visitors noted the town looked like a large timber yard due to all the construction. War had been declared against England on 18 June 1812 and he was not looking forward to what the future might hold. Monthly Militia drills were primarily social events and he knew the militia was not prepared to fight professional British soldiers. Neither was he convinced the war was necessary. His uncle was able to sell his wheat and sheep to Canada in spite of the embargo Congress had placed on foreign trade.

Most importantly, he would need to give up his job as a farm hand for his uncle leaving Lucy with no income to raise Abel, Mathew, their little sister and the new baby. One of those pesky Irish immigrants coming over the Canadian border would snap up his place and that would be the end of his position. Jacob was not afraid of fighting; his father and 15 Fuller cousins had been Soldiers of the Revolution. It was not fear of the British that troubled him. It was the country's weak condition and not having his own land to support his young family. Jacob was more concerned about surviving from one day to the next. He had to admit that Whitehall was not the best place for someone in his circumstances.

Severe floods on Wood Creek and the Poultney River in the spring of 1810 had wiped out farmland and crops. The village suffered from inflation, disease, mammoth mosquitoes and was generally described as "…being then a very immoral place." (Ensign, 1878) Settlers rushing to New York were driving up the price of land. Many of the young men in the valley were taking their families and moving to the new state of Ohio and the Conneticut Reserve lands where land was cheap and Indians still hunted along the shores of Lake Erie. Enoch Fuller, two years his senior, had left in 1805, married, and his wife, "Happy" gave birth to the first child in the town of Ashtabula in 1806. (Upton, 1910) His kinfolk who had bought farmland in 1785 from the confiscated lands of Philip Skene, had for the most part sold their property and moved to western New York, Ohio, and Pennsylvania. Maybe he should too. He would talk to Lucy about it.

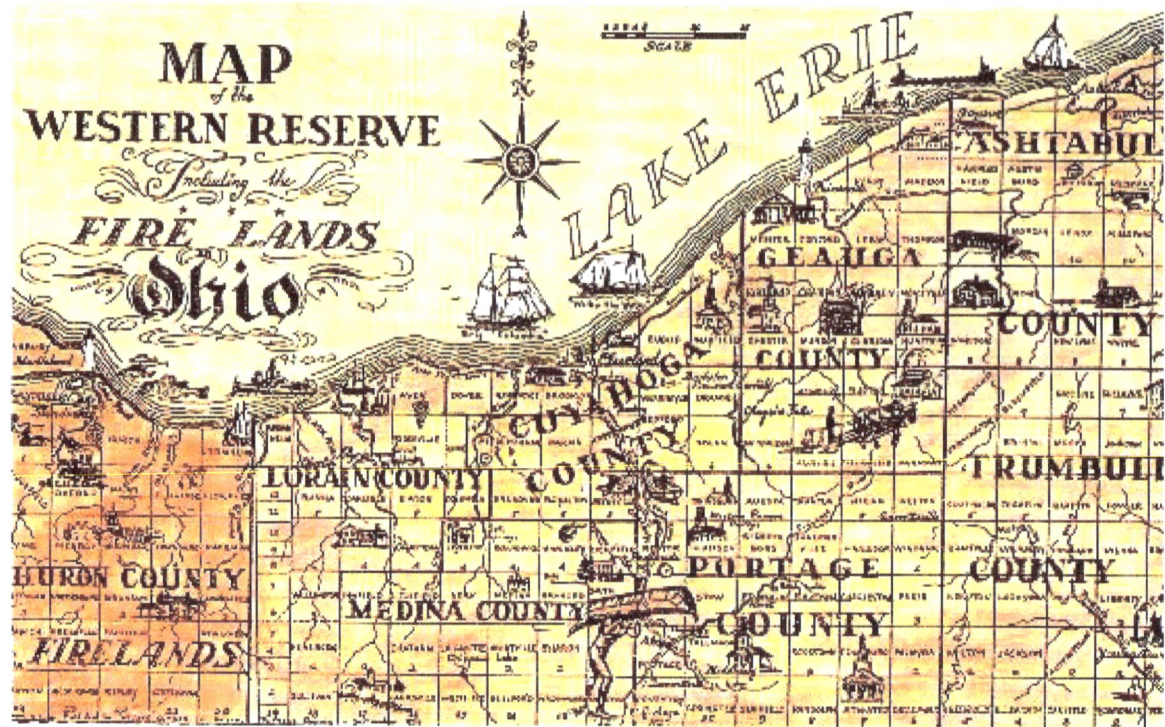

Genealogists Mary Nussbaum and Laurel Fuller Carnahan report that Jacob and sons arrived in Ohio soon after the birth of Samuel, who presumably stayed behind with his mother, Lucy. (documentation unknown) It is said the family came from Buffalo by open boat around 7 Dec 1812. The question is, where did Jacob and the boys find shelter from the icy winds of Lake Erie? Did they stay in Kirkland with Enoch and Happy? Or, perhaps with Thomas Fuller who had arrived in June of 1812 (at the beginning of the War of 1812). Thomas was a millwright who made mill-stones from granite boulders. (Crary, 1893) Or did they travel with Mathew Fuller from Whitehall to Painesville?

Jacob appears to have been one of many settlers who came west with neither money nor property, hoping to buy land and make a permanent home for his family. It is likely he worked for other farmers from 1812 until purchasing his own property in 1823. We do know the family moved from Painesville to Brecksville in 1817. (Johnson, 1879)

The War of 1812 ended 18 Feb 1815 bringing financial ruin and a depression to the young American country. *"The sudden ending of the War of 1812 ruined many who had purchased supplies for the army. The war had destroyed commerce. The national debt was a hundred million dollars. Banks all over the country were obliged to suspend specie payment. Men in New England and Middle states were out of work. Land in Ohio was cheap, and a great western movement set in this year."* (Johnson, 1879)

*"…houses and barns were of logs. The inhabitants were many of them very poor, having exchanged their small estates with the land proprietors of the east for lands here, with just money enough to transport themselves and their families, and to purchase a year's provisions in the wild and untamed region,"* wrote Rev. Mr. Hall in 1811. *"…the farmer found but little pay for his crops, as there was no market…and money was very scarce. The prices at this time of grain raised from land were one dollar for wheat, fifty cents for corn, twenty-five cents for oats, four cents per pound for pork while salt…cost four dollars per barrel."* **(Williams, 1878)**

*During the war the prices of produce were tripled. The increased circulation of money made everything seem very profitable to the producer. But the war closed. Merchants had contracted for large amounts, but found the demands for their supplies had ceased. The circulation of war money ceased. Property had to be disposed of. Prices fell to one-fourth of what they had been. A great stagnation of business followed. Business men were driven to great straits, and some of them to bankruptcy. The war had stopped migration also, and there was no market for produce. …at this time the farmers, in order to sell their grain and so save transportation, resorted to the expedient of reducing the grains, such as rye and corn, to whisky…many distilleries were erected…high wines to an eastern market…the whisky itself was shippped west."* **(ibid)**

Thomas Fuller moved to Fullertown (Russell township, Geauga County) where he settled on a 200 acre lot (at $4 per acre) in 1820. By 1821 he had built a home and a gristmill (with partner Mr. Allison). Mr. Allison sold out before the mill was complete and Thomas ran the mill day and night, paying off his debts. He then built a sawmill and cardingworks. He later built a woolen-mill, where he worked into his nineties. **(Sidneyrigdon.com, 1880)**

From Painesville, Jacob and Lucy moved to Brecksville (Cuyahoga County) in 1817. **(Ohio Pioneer Women, reference unverifiable).** The family's arrival was also documented in the Brecksville Township History, *"Jacob Fuller and his sons, Abel, Mathew, Calvin, Quartus, Willis and Samuel, Warren Cole, … were all early settlers in the northern and western part of the township."* By 1820 there were a number of Fullers living in the Cayahoga, Lake, Asthtabula, Trumbull County area.

Fullers living in the Cayahoga, Lake, Asthtabula, Trumbull County area:

>Jacob Fuller (Cuyahoga Co.) from NY, b. about 1785
>Enoch Fuller (Ashtabula Co.) from NY, b. about 1781, son of Matthew
>Amasa Fuller (Willoughby, Lake Co.)
>Amisa Fuller (Cuyahoga Co.) b. before 1775, son of Asa Fuller
>Isaac Fuller ( Newburgh, Cuyahoga Co.) b. before 1800, son of Matthew
>Joseph Fuller (Geauga Co.) from Munson, Mass, b. 1758. Son of Nathaniel Fuller
>Mathew Fuller (Geauga Co.) from New York, son of Aaron Fuller (1711)
>Simeon Fuller (Willoughby, Lake Co.) from Bolton, Ct, b. 1761, son of Daniel
>Thomas Fuller (Geauga Co.)
>Rebecca (Fuller) Carter (Cleveland, Cuyahoga Co.) from Warren, CT
>Howard Fuller (Cleveland, Cuyahoga Co.) from Warren, CT
>Davis Fuller (Cleveland, Cuyahoga Co.) from Hartland, CT
>William Fuller (Warrensville Hts., Cuyahoga Co.) from Mass, b. 1745
>William A. Fuller (Strongsville, Cuyahoga Co.) from NY, son of Matthew

*"Of the first settlers, some men walked the entire way from Connecticut; some rode horseback part way, sharing the horse with others; some rode in ox carts; some drove oxen; some came part way by land and the rest by water; some came on sleds in mid-winter; some plowed through the mud of spring, or endured the heat of summer; some had bleeding feet, and some serious illnesses. Sometimes it was bride and a groom who started alone; sometimes it was a husband, wife and children; sometimes it was a group of neighbors who made the party. Children were born on the way, and people of all ages died and were buried where they died. But after they came, their experiences were almost identical.*

*Most of the travelers came in family or neighborhood groups, with an ox cart for the baggage, and a horse or two. There was seldom place for all to ride and they took turn about. A large percent came by horseback. Sometimes a woman would ride, carrying a baby and utensils for cooking, while the husband would walk, leading another horse on which was piled the baggage. Often a husband and wife, newly married, would ride horses, or one horse, to the new home. Sometimes men used boats as far as streams were navigatable, walking the rest of the way. Sometimes men walked all the way. Sometimes women came in pairs without men, walking the entire distance. Sometimes women carried babies on their backs while the husbands carried provisions on his. When it came night they would sleep on the ground, with no covering if it were pleasant, under the trees or large pieces of bark stuck on poles, if it were rainy. Record is given of women who came alone (except as they would fall in with parties now and then), carrying a baby or leading a child. In this latter case the trip was exceedingly hard. In the beginning such a traveler was in civilization, where she could easily find shelter and lodging. However, as she proceeded, and grew more weary and more lonesome, hamlets were farther apart, until houses almost disappeared. It is recorded that several women carried their babies in their aprons all the way from New England. The apron was worn almost as much as the dress, colored cottons for hard work, white for home dress-up, and among the wealthy silk for visiting. They were used for many purposes for which we would never think of using them today.*

*When women came alone it was usually because they were exceedingly poor and had inherited land in the new country, or because the husband had preceded them to prepare a place for them. Many a pioneer mother, when she reached the land belonging to her or to her husband, saw the wild country, remembered her abiding place "back home", covered her face with her hands, sat down on the fresh hewn logs, or made her way into the forests, and gave way to her feelings in floods of tears. As soon as this disappointment was over, she turned her attention to her duty. If any women, anywhere, in all the wide world, ever did the courageous things, the right things it was the women who came to New Connecticut and helped to transform it from wilderness to one of the most prosperous places of the world. As there were some women who came in rather comfortable ox-carts, so there were some women who had homes awaiting them, but this percent was so small that it is hardly to be considered."* (Upton, 1910)

On 22 May 1823, Jacob Fuller's mortgage was recorded for a 203 acre parcel of land purchased from Leonard Case, located in the Case Western Reserve in Brecksville, Cuyahoga, Ohio. Jacob paid $10.90 in back taxes due on the property and the property was his. In September of the same year, Jacob sold 50 acres of the parcel for a sum of $300. The original tract is shown in red cross hatch on the figure below. The yellow parcel of 79.21 acres is the last parcel Jacob owned prior to moving to Putnam County.

**First land purchase of Jacob Fuller, 203 acres in Brecksville, Cuyahoga, OH, 22 May 1823.**

In 2011, Jacob's former property is the site of many luxury homes with deep wooded lots. An index of his land deeds in Cuyahoga County, Ohio is on the following page. Often his wife (Lucy or Mary) was a co-signer.

A home site on Jacob Fuller's Original plat (April 2011)　　　　Photo by K. L. Houk

The land in Brecksville Township was hilly and wooded, with only small areas flat enough for farming purposes. Yet, Jacob raised his family there from 1818 until moving west to Putnam County, OH in 1853. His only known venture into public office was as a Township Trustee in 1830. The New England settlers brought with them to Ohio the civic organizational structure of New England, including the position of "Overseer of the Poor," whose job it was to serve "writs" upon people of poor financial and character status, ordering them to leave the township. (No documentation has yet been found of our ancestors being requested to leave town while living in Ohio.)

Jacob had two wives. Lucy Evans came with him from New York. She co-signed many of the land deeds and is shown in the 1830 census (white female age 30-39). Her "mark" on documents disappears after June 1830 and is replaced by that of Mary Cole Fuller, following her marriage to Jacob in 1833 (Source: Marriage Certificate). Mary Cole is most likely the widow of

BEWARE CUYAHOGA COUNTY RESIDENTS There are organizations soliciting, at an excessive cost, requests from you to purchase a Certified Deed which proves your title was transferred to you. If your deed was recorded in the Cuyahoga County Recorder

search of **Jacob Fuller** return 23 result(s)

(Seller) to Lot (Buyer)

| APN | Doc. Type | Name | Assoc. Name | Date Recorded | Reference | Legal Description | Book/Page |
|---|---|---|---|---|---|---|---|
| 182305220001 | MORT | LEONARD CASE Range 12, 5, 19 | JACOB FULLER 203 Ac | 5/22/1823 1/c.90 | Sale for taxes twen | | 4/456 |
| 182310020002 | DEED | JACOB FULLER | DANIEL GREEN | 10/2/1823 | | " | 4/531 |
| 182611210002 | DEED | JACOB FULLER | ISAAC MORGAN | 11/21/1826 | | " | 6/314 |
| 182701280001 | DEED | THOMAS WEBB | JACOB FULLER | 1/28/1827 | | " | 6/381 |
| 182906120003 | DEED | JACOB FULLER | ALVAH DARROW | 6/12/1829 | | CLEVELAND " | 8/220 |
| 182909160003 | DEED | ALVAH DARROW | JACOB FULLER | 9/16/1829 | | " | 8/307 |
| 183006100006 | DEED | JACOB FULLER | ALVAH DARROW | 6/10/1830 | | " | 9/110 |
| 183006110001 | DEED | JACOB FULLER | ALVAH DARROW | 6/11/1830 | | " | 9/110 |
| 183310180003 | DEED | JACOB FULLER | ABEL FULLER | 10/18/1833 | | | 13/21 |
| 183312160001 | DEED | JOSEPH BRECK | JACOB FULLER | 12/16/1833 | | | 13/195 |
| 183610050001 | DEED | TITUS STREET | JACOB FULLER | 10/5/1836 | | | 21/26 |
| 183706120004 | DEED | JACOB FULLER | JOHN DERR | 6/12/1837 | | Polly | 22/466 |
| 183706120005 | DEED | JASPER FULLER | JACOB FULLER | 6/12/1837 | | Betsy Mary | 22/467 |
| 183712040004 | DEED | JACOB FULLER | OLIVE SPARLING | 12/4/1837 | | Mary | 23/661 |
| 184308030001 | DEED | JACOB FULLER | JOHN CARY | 8/3/1843 | | | 32/815 |
| 184310210005 | DEED | JACOB FULLER | ELIJAH PECK | 10/21/1843 | | | 33/119 |
| 184410160003 | DEED | JOHN ROBISON | JACOB FULLER | 10/16/1844 | | MAIN | 34/498 |
| 184508220005 | DEED | THOMAS MATHEWS | JACOB FULLER | 8/22/1845 | | MAIN | 35/624 |
| 184701120007 | DEED | HULSEY HESTON | JACOB FULLER | 1/12/1847 | | DUNHAM | 38/688 |
| 185203200007 | DEED | JACOB FULLER | RICHARD SMITH | 3/20/1852 | | MAIN Mary | 55/193 |
| 185208310005 | DEED | JACOB FULLER | WILLIAM WHITE | 8/31/1852 | | Mary | 58/132 |
| 185212080002 | DEED | JACOB FULLER | ELIZABETH BADGER | 12/8/1852 | | DUNHAM Mary | 59/277 |
| 185304050002 | DEED | JACOB FULLER | JOHN BRECK Lot 8 79.21 Ac | 4/5/1853 #1750 | 4/5/2003 | Mary | 61/427 |

©2008 Cuyahoga County Recorder's Office. Click to read our Legal Disclaimer about our documents.
Click here to read our Policy Statement.
Developed and Designed By Cuyahoga County Recorder's Office.

Jacob's good friend and neighbor in 1830, Warren Cole. (Warren is reported to have died from a "bilious fever" in 1828, (Brecksville Centennial, p. 57) although he is shown living adjacent Jacob in the 1830 census, so either the date is wrong or he died of another ailment after 1830. All give their birthplace as New York in census documents.) Jacob had at least 14 children, as discerned from census records, yet it is quite possible he could have had children that died between census dates. The 1840 census show he absorbed at least one daughter from his marriage to Mary Cole. It is also difficult to determine exact family relationships because early census records did not report the relationships of persons living in a household unit.

> Jacob Fuller to Mary Cole
>
> State of Ohio Cuyahoga County ss. This certifies that on the fourth day of July AD 1833 Jacob Fuller and Mary Cole both of Brecksville were legally joined in marriage by me a Justice of the Peace in and for the county of Cuyahoga. Given under my hand this tenth day of Sept. AD 1833. William S. Green Justice Peace

Jacob and Mary Fuller sold their last parcel of 79.21 acres for $1,750 in April 1853 and headed to Putnam County in northwestern Ohio where they had bought 80 acres for $700 earlier in the year (Feb 1853, Putnam Co. deed). By October they apparently "swapped" some land, selling 50 acres on October 9th and then buying 40 acres from Abel & Catherine Fuller on October 10th (Putnam Co. deeds).

1.1.1.1 Abel had preceded his father to Putnam County, purchasing 120 acres of government-owned land on 22 April 1835 for $150 (about $1.20/acre). The parcel (*"the south half of the northwest quarter and the southwest quarter of the northeast quarter of Section Number 15, Township Number One South and Range Number Seven East"*) was obtained under a Congressional Act to extend the Miami-Erie Canal from Fort Wayne and Cincinnati to Lake Erie. Money from the sale of government lands went to fund construction of a canal system to provide transportation for both people and cargo throughout the state.

An "original settler" (after the Ottawa Indians) in the "Black Swamp" of Putnam County, Abel was one of only seven voters in Pleasant Township in 1834. A good hunting dog was worth $100 and settlers sold wolf scalps to the government for $3-$4 to pay their taxes. Putnam County was located in a swamp; 30-40 miles wide from Fort Wayne, Indiana on the west to the

Sandusky River in Ohio (120 miles). Scooped out by glaciers, the area was muddy and almost impassable. A 1837 poem in the Maumee City Express described it this way:

*There's a funeral every day,
without a hearse or pall;
They tuck them in the ground
with breeches, coat and all.*

Settlers bought (or were given if they could not afford to buy) seedling apple trees from John Chapman ("Johnny Appleseed") who had a nursery near Fort Findlay and paddled the waterways selling his trees.

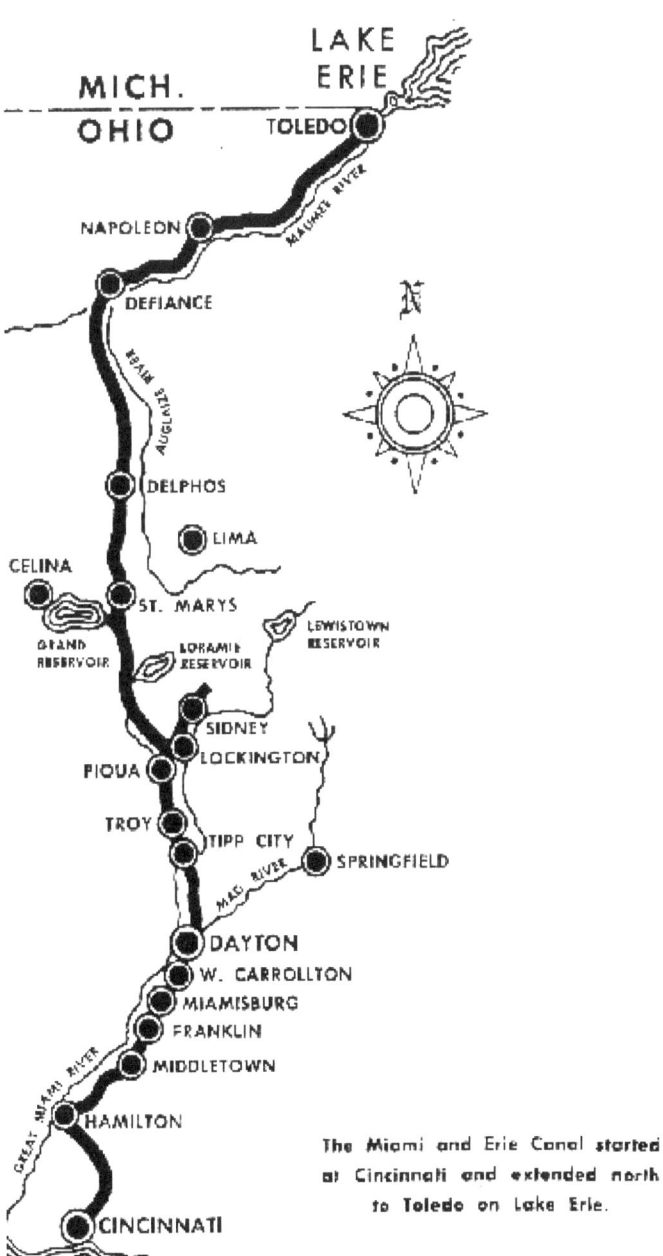

The Miami and Erie Canal started at Cincinnati and extended north to Toledo on Lake Erie.

Life was hard. Putnam County deeds show Abel sold 80 acres for $122 and an additional 80 acres for $52.17 on 22 Oct 1840. Few deed transactions were found due to a flood at the County Court House in 1866, destroying many city documents. Few were recreated, making it difficult to obtain primary documents. Jacob and Mary arrived in Putnam County just before the Cholera epidemic of 1854. They found the mosquitoes *"so bad in the warm months that heavy clothing had to be worn for protection which made the labor of clearing the trees and under-growth even more sweltering. To keep the mosquitoes at bay at night settlers kept smudge pots in their cabins....Late summer saw the onset of malarial illness called ague, which led to soaring fever, deep chills and violent shaking which went on for days or even weeks. It was not unusual for entire families to lay inside their cabins and shake uncontrollably."* **(The Great Black Swamp by Jim Mollenkopf)**

By 1850, Dutch settlers in southwestern Putnam County brought their engineering skills from the lowlands of Holland, introducing the concept of draining the swamp. Ohio passed a law in 1859 authorizing the levy of heavy farm taxes to fund the digging of public ditches to drain the swamp. Farmers also buried inverted wooden troughs and clay tile to underdrain the fields. By 1880, more than fifty tile factories supplied tile to free the heavy black loam, turning it into one of the most productive agricultural regions in the country. (see, "The Great Black Swamp by Carolyn V. Platt; www.newbermenhistory.org) The value of Jacob's real estate rose to $4,000 in the 1870 census, the last known record of him. A death certificate was not issued in Putnam County for Jacob Fuller during 1872, the reported year of his death. Similarly, the death of Mary Cole Fuller, Jacob's second wife, can only be estimated as sometime between the 1860 and 1870 census. No public records of her death have been found as of 1 Oct 2011.

Rich farming lands of Putnam County, once a part of The Great Black Swamp (April, 2011 Photo by K. L. Houk)

The Miami and Erie Canal, extending 249 miles from Toledo to Cincinnati, Ohio, was built between 1825 and 1845. The canal had 19 aqueducts, guard locks, and 103 lift locks.** *The series of 105 canal locks raised canal boats 395 feet above Lake Erie, and 513 above the Ohio River at Cincinnati, Ohio. Each canal lock was 90 feet long by 15 feet. The peak of the Miami and Erie Canal at the "Loramie Summit" extended 21 miles from Lock 1-N in New Bremen, Ohio, to lock 1-S in Lockington north of Piqua, Ohio. The entire canal system was 301.49 miles long and cost $8,062,680.07.

During the construction of the Miami and Erie Canal, it was a center of disease, and drunken violence. Irish immigrants, convicts, and local farmers used picks, shovels and wheelbarrows to relocate the dirt and clay. This dawn to dusk labor brought in a wage of 30 cents a day.

By its completion in 1845, the Miami and Erie Canal was soon to have competition by the expanding railway system. From 1850 to 1860, the railway system in Ohio went from 375 to 2946 miles of track. In the 1860's the City of Cincinnati received a 3/4 mile outlet of the Miami and Erie Canal for street and sewer expansion. During that same era, Toledo was given several miles of the canal for similar purposes. In 1861, the Ohio legislature passed a law allowing the leasing of canals for a ten-year term to a private company for the annual rent of $20,075. The lease included maintenance mandates of the canals; however, the law lacked conditions to provide documentation of the canal's value and condition at the time of the lease. During this period, the canals deteriorated greatly. In late 1877, the lessees refused to pay the rent of the prior six months.

During the active life of the Miami and Erie Canal, canal boats made transportation of passengers and goods possible from Lake Erie to the Ohio River. Passengers fees were 2 to 3 cents per mile, with the hauling of freight costing 2 cents per mile per ton with fees going down to 1.5 cents on trips over 100 miles. The canal boats traveled 4 to 5 miles per hour. Canal minimum construction standards included: 1) 4 ft. water depth; 2) 40 ft. wide at water level; 3) A 10 ft. wide towpath in addition to mandated outer slopes; 4) All slopes are 4-1/2 ft. horizontal to 4 ft. perpendicular; 5) Canal Boats could be up 14 ft. wide

Ohio Canals prior to the Civil War returned to the State nearly seven million dollars in net receipts. The canals were also a major factor in Ohio's major population growth, wealth, and power. In fact, the population expansion in Ohio jumped 68% between 1830 and 1840. Indirect effects of the Canals in Ohio include raising the prices of labor and products within Ohio, which promoted the growth of industries such as agriculture and mining. One such example was the price of a bushel of wheat grown in central Ohio, went from 50 to 75 cents.

References: Marker at St. Marys' Memorial park; Marker located in downtown New Bremen; " History of the Ohio Canals", J.E. Hagerty, copyright 1905; "Pathways of Progress", David W. Bowman, copyright 1943; Map of Ohio Canals, prepared by Capt. Hiram M. Chittenden, Corps of Engineers, U.S.A ; "Vol.III The Passing of the Frontier, Ohio State Archaeological and Historical Society, copyright 1941; See, www.hiking.ohiotrail.com/trails/canal-history.htm

Canal markers near Putnam County

By 1888, Jacob Fuller's community (before his reported death in 1872) of Columbus Grove, Putnam County, OH had five churches and a school population of 509. Businesses in the village were: J. F. McBride (mfg. jeans, blankets, etc – 8 employees); Buckeye Stave Co. – 60 employees; J. S. Lehman & Co. (drain tile – 6 employees); M. Pease (flour, etc. – 5 employees); Crawford & Co. (lumber – 4 employees); Perkins & Allen (doors, sash, etc. – 10 employees); J. F. Jones (axe-handles – 15 employees); Henderson & Light (flour, etc. – 5 employees); W. R. Kaufman (drain tile – 6 employees); and the *Putnam County Vidette* newspaper.*(State Report, 1887)*

Records of Jacob's children are also intermittent. His eldest son, Abel B. Fuller, will be detailed in Section 2. The compiler of this book is indebted to fellow genealogists Lola Partrain (for information on the lineage of Orphelia (Orpha) Fuller (1823-1865)) and Stefani Ferguson (for information on the lineage of Joseph Clinton Fuller (1872-1953)).

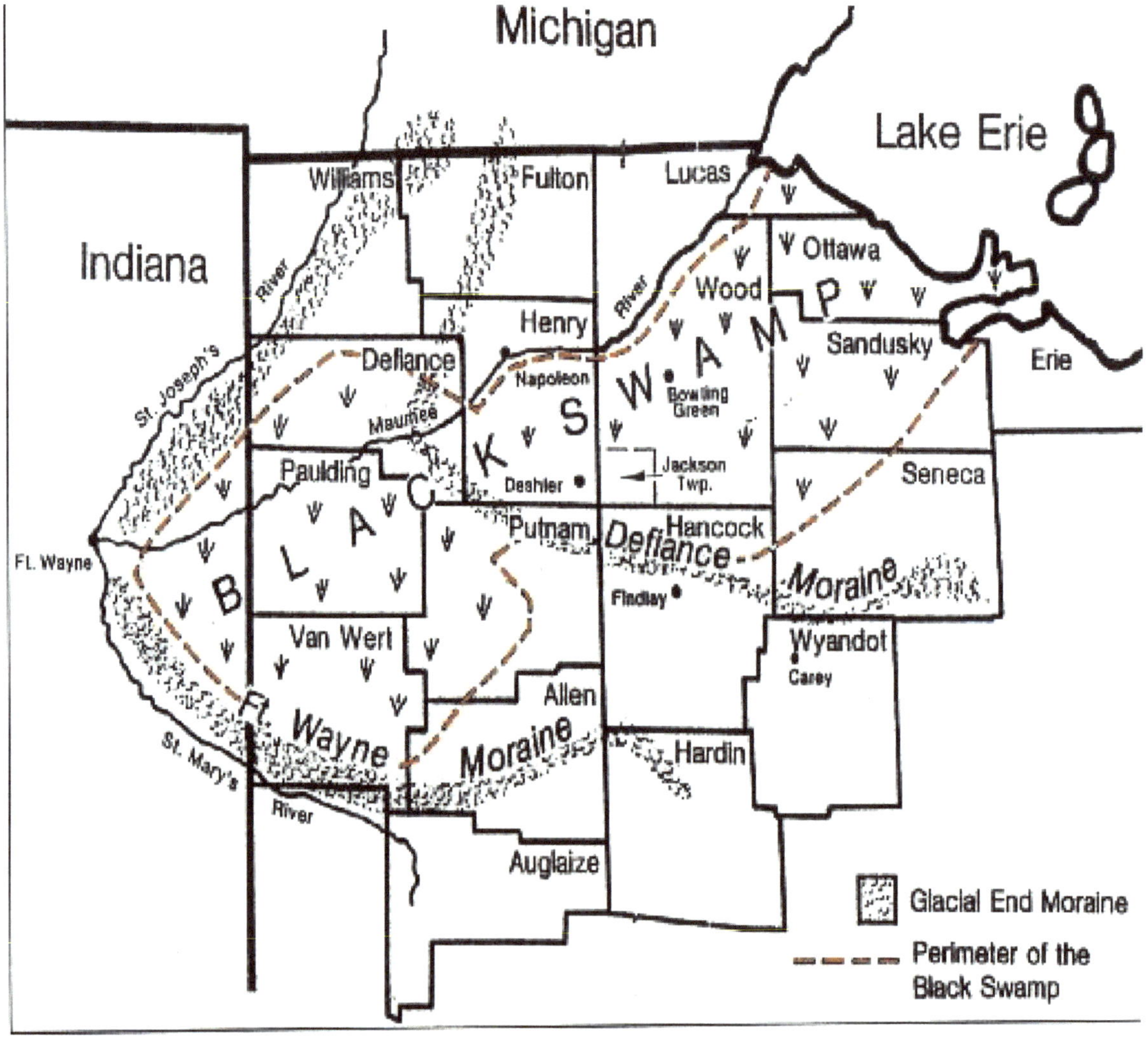
Michigan
Lake Erie
Indiana
Williams
Fulton
Lucas
Ottawa
Wood
Henry
Defiance
Napoleon
Bowling Green
Sandusky
Erie
Maumee
River
St. Joseph's
Paulding
Deshler
Jackson Twp.
Seneca
Ft. Wayne
Putnam
Hancock
Defiance
Moraine
Findlay
B L A C K S W A M P
Van Wert
Wyandot
Carey
Allen
Ft. Wayne
Moraine
Hardin
St. Mary's
River
Auglaize
Glacial End Moraine
Perimeter of the Black Swamp

# Jacob Fuller's Children

| Name | Occupation | Highest Worth | Spouse(s) | Children | Residences | Death & Burial |
|---|---|---|---|---|---|---|
| Abel B Fuller (1805-1856) | Farmer (owned land) | $1000 (1850) | (Ms's: Cole, Mayberry, & Pence) | Thirteen | NY, Cuyahoga & Putnam Co., OH | June 1856 unknown |
| Matthew (1809-1859) | Farmer (owned land) By 1850 he is listed as a shoemaker | (1850) Real estate valued at $100 | Elizabeth A. Durfee | Five | NY, Cuyahoga & Putnam Co., OH | 1859: Wisely Cemetery, Pleasant, Putnam Co., OH |
| Anna (1811-Before 1870) | Married to Farmer | Not given | Elisha Crandall | Seven | NY, CT, & Cuyahoga Co., OH | unknown |
| Samuel (1812-1890) | Farmer | $2300 | Eunice M Ashley | Seven | Vt/NY, Cuyahoga & Paulding Co., OH | 18 Mar 1890: Sherman Cemetery, Paulding Co., OH |
| Quartas (1817-1860) | Laborer | Not given | Elizabeth Norton | Four | Cuyahoga & Putnam Co's., OH | unknown |
| Calvin (1819-1878) | Farmer (owned land) | $800 (1870) | Susannah Campbell | Three | Cuyahoga, Ashtabula & Paulding Co's., OH | 16 July 1878: Prairie Chapel Brown, Paulding, OH |
| Orphelia (1823-1865) | Married to Farmer | $900 (1860) | Jabez Devatus/ Joe Belden | Eight | Ohio, Illinois, Texas & MO | Abt 1862, Sherman, Grayson, TX |
| Willis (1828-1900?) | Laborer & Farmer | $800 (1870) | Never Married, Lived with Calvin's Widow | None | Cuyahoga, Ashtabula, Paulding & Putnam Co's., OH | After 1880 |
| Cynthia (1834- | Married to Day Laborer | Not given | James Asbury Elliott | Five | Cuyahoga & Putnam Co's., OH | After 1900 |
| Maria (1837- | unknown | unknown | unknown | unknown | Cuyahoga Co, OH | unknown |
| Jacob E. (1838-dbd) | Farmer | $4560 (1870) w/Jacob Sr. | Francis M. Green | Two girls given up for adoption in 1871, after Mother's death | Cuyahoga & Putnam Co., OH, KS | Moved to KS in 1871, death records not found (TBD) |
| Harry (Rev) (1840-1928) | Farmer & Minister (owned land) | Not given | Polly Carnahan | Five | Cuyahoga & Paulding Co., Oh | 27 Dec 1923 |

# ABEL B. FULLER (1805 – 1856) (See Section 2)

## MATTHEW FULLER (1809 – 1859)

The second child of Jacob Fuller and Lucy Evans, Matthew appears to have left Brecksville and headed to Putnam County soon after, or perhaps with, Abel and Roxanne. He purchased 80 acres of public land (*the east half of the northwest quarter of Section 10, in Township One, South, of Range Seven East*) from the Lima, OH land office on 15 March 1837. He married Elizabeth Abigail Durfee on Dec. 10th of that year in Pleasant Township.

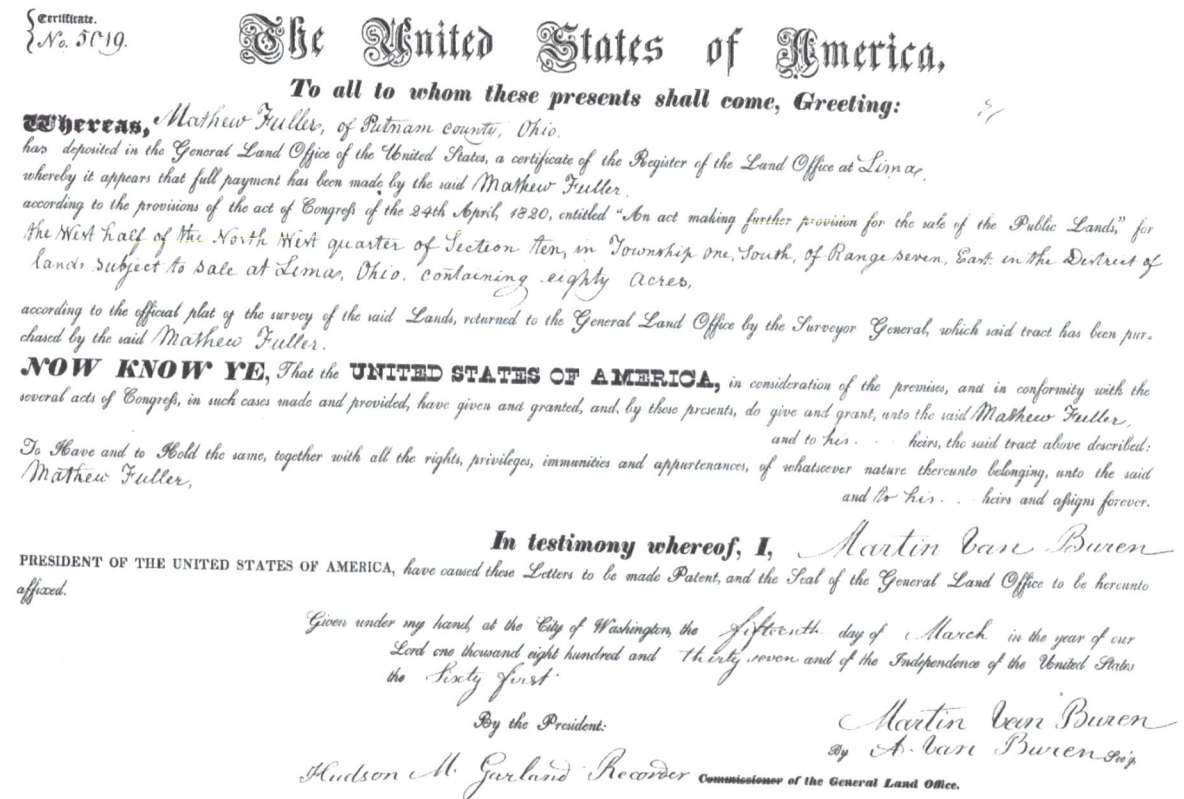

Matthew and Abigail had five known children. All three boys served in the Civil War, with Reubin Martin being killed at the Battle of Corinth, MS, July 1862 while serving with the 14th Regiment of the Ohio Volunteer Infantry. In the 1850 census, Matthew's occupation is given as "shoemaker" with real estate valued at $100; indicating he had sold his farmland. Deeds from 19 Mar 1839, 11 Aug 1839, 28 Aug 1840, and 26 Jan 1850 remain on file at the Putnam County Courthouse showing some of Matthew's land transactions. He died in 1859 and is buried in Wisely Cemetery, Putnam Co. with Abigail, who lived until 1880. Mathew's children were: Jacob Willis (1839-1918); Reuben Martin (1841-1862); William Robert (b. 1844); Rosetta D. (b. 1854); and Mary L. (b. 1857).

## ANNA FULLER CRANDALL (1811 – died before 1870)

Anna was born to Jacob and Lucy in 1811, before they left Whitehall, NY. She traveled to Brecksville, Ohio, as a child and there married Elisha Crandall, farmer, on 12 Feb 1827. Seven known children were born to the couple. They are living in Brecksville, near Jacob and Lucy in 1830, with two children under age 10. Elisha was born in Conneticut and it is possible the couple was living there during the 1840 census. By 1850 they had settled in Saybrook Township, Ashtabula County, OH. In 1860, they are living separately; Elisha (63) is living in Geneva Township with a farmer by the name of Jennings, and Anna with daughters Caroline and Maranda is still living in Saybrook. William H. Crandall, Anna's oldest son, appears to have spent his life in Saybrook, working as a ship carpenter, and married to Henrietta. There is no record of children. In 1900, he is living with his brother-in-law, Stephen Seamans in Saybrook.

Anna Fuller and Elisha Crandall are known to have the following children; William N Crandall (b. 1827), Lois Ann Crandall (1832-1913), Samuel Crandall, (b. 1839), Caroline Crandall (1841-1916), Marena Crandall, (b. 1844), Maranda Crandall, (b. 1846), and Zachara T. Crandall, (b. 1848).
(source: genforum.genealogy.com)

## SAMUEL FULLER (1812 – 1890)
Samuel Fuller was born just prior to Jacob and Lucy's move from Whitehall, NY to Ohio. He grew up in Brecksville and followed his future wife to Bond Co., IL, where they married on 18 Dec 1838. Samuel began farming in Illinois, buying 40 acres in Bond County on 1 Nov 1839. He moved to Coles County, IL, purchasing 40 acres from the U.S. Government Land Office in 1840 and 85 acres in 1849. The couple's children were born in Illinois; Willis A. (1839-1928), Martha A. (1840-1841), Isaac (1842-1844), Albert (1844-1917), and Happalonia (1847-1939).

Twin girls born in 1851 died the same year. Paulding County deeds show Samuel purchased 80 acres on 30 June 1858 and an additional 40 acres on 6 July 1871. Samuel's family differed from that of Abel, in deeding land to their surviving children (such as Happalonia, who appears to have remained unmarried) prior to death. (see Section 2)

Samuel's son Willis lost an arm in the Civil War at the battle of Atlanta, GA (Pvt., 68th Regiment, Company C, Ohio Infantry, 1861-1865) but returned to marry Nancy Agnes Burt (1848-1923) and raise ten children. They were; Ethel M. Fuller (1886-19667), Essie A. Fuller (1888-1955), Glennie E. Fuller (b.1893), Marshall Dewey Fuller (1897-1942), Aden Cloyde Fuller (1900-1982), Clyde R. Fuller (1902-1944), Floyd G. Fuller, (b. 1905), Lola Merle Fuller (1908-1918), Lynn Fuller (b. 1909), and Lawrence Albert Fuller (1915-1935) Following Nancy's death in 1923, Willis remarried Ms. Bessie Harger in 1935.

Albert also served in the Civil War (Pvt., 68th Regiment, Company C, Ohio Infantry). He married Esther A. Baird in 1870 and they had two children who survived, George B. Fuller (1875-1940) and Elsie Eudora Fuller (1880-1960) After Esther's death in 1903, Albert remarried Ms. Eva Dora Rathburn, born in 1857. He died in Fort Wayne, Indiana, on 23 June 1917.

It is from Samuel's obituary (right) and census records we are able to determine the family did originally come from Whitehall, NY. Samuel consistently calls it Whitehall, Vermont; which indicates the family was involved in the bitter boundary disputes between New York and Vermont before and after the Revolutionary War.

The obituary errs in stating that Samuel's father (Jacob) served in the Revolutionary War (Jacob was born in 1785). It should read his "grandfather" was in the Revolutionary War.

> Samuel Fuller was the son of Jacob and Lucy (Evans) Fuller and was born in Whitehall Vermont Nov 18 1812, He was married in Illnois Dec 19 1837 to Eunice M Ashley daughter of Isaac and Eunice (Levett) Ashley, she was born Mar 17 1817 in Genesee Co,N Y Her mother died in Cuyahoga Co Oh and her father died in Ill.
> Their family consisted of seven children Willis Mar 31 1839; Martha A Oct 15, 1840 died Apr 20 1841; Isaac A July 9 1842, died July 10 1844; Albert Sept 10 1844, Happalonia Aug 3 1847, Ellen Ada and Ellen Adell twins born Sep 27 1851, Ellen Ada died Oct 17 1851 and Ellen Adell Oct 29 1851. Mr Fuller's parents are both deceased. His sons Willis and Albert were in the Civil War. Willis\ lost an amr July 22 1864 in front of Atlanta they both remained in Service until the close of the war. His father was in the Revolutionary War. Sam is a farmer in Brown Twp, Paulding Co. Samuel died Mar 18 1890, and his burial was in Sherman Cemetery. Eunice M died April 11 1901, Happalonia died Mar 18 1939. All buried in Sherman Cemetery on family plot.

The Historical Hand Atlas of Paulding County, Ohio, 1882, describes Samuel below:
> "SAMUEL FULLER – was one of the pioneers of this county, having settled in Brown township in 1853; at that time there was no road from his place to Charloe, and he had to carry his grain on his back to the mill. He was married in Illinois, December 19,1837 to Eunice M. Ashley, daughter of Isaac and Eunice (Levette) Ashley. She was born in Genesee county, New York, March 8, 1817; her father died in Illinois; her mother died in Cuyahoga county, Ohio. Mr. Fuller was born in Whitehall, Vermont, November 18, 1812. Their family consists of: Willis, born March 31, 1839; Martha A., October 15, 1840, died April 20, 1841; Isaac A., July 9, 1842, died July 10, 1844; Albert, September 10, 1844; Happalonia, August 8, 1847; Ellen Ada and Ellen Adell, twins, September 27, 1851, Ellen Ada died October 17, 1851, and Ellen Adell died October 29, 1851. Mr. Fuller's parents were Jacob and Lucy (Evans) Fuller; both are deceased. His sons Willis and Albert were in the war of 1861. Willis lost an arm, July 22, 1861,in front of Atlanta; they both remained in service until the close of the war. His father was a teamster in the war of 1812, and his grandfather was in the Revolutionary war. Mr. Fuller is a farmer. Address; Oakwood, Paulding county, Ohio."

## QUARTAS FULLER (1817 – before 1852)

Quartas Fuller, later spelled Cortez Fuller by genealogists, also went to Putnam County in the 1830s, most likely to be a farm laborer for his brothers. He married Elizabeth (Betsy) Norton on 20 Feb 1838 and the 1850 census shows they had four children at that time; Sylvia Fuller (b. 1843), Rosanna Fuller (1844-1916); Clarissa or Melissa Fuller (b. 1846), and Garrison Fuller, (b. 1849). They were living in Blanchard Township, Putnam County and Quartas worked as a laborer. Quartas/Cortez appears to have died shortly after 1850. Betsy married Lewis Sigafoose, a farmer from Virginia on 9 Nov 1852 and by the 1860 census they were farming in Butler Township, Miami County, IN. They owned no real estate and their net worth was $400. Daughter Clarissa remained with neighbors Elisha (a merchant) and Abigale Stout in Blanchard Township, Putnam County, Ohio. The 1970 census shows that husband Lewis had become a Butcher. Again, there is no ownership of real estate shown, and Lewis had a net worth of $150. The family does not appear in the 1880 census, but Betsy is shown as widowed and living with her youngest children or perhaps grandchildren on a farm in Cherokee County, KS in 1885. Record of Quartas' death has not yet been found.

The rich fields of Blanchard Township, Putnam County, Ohio (source: Wikipedia-public domain)

## CALVIN FULLER ( 1819 – 1878)

Born in Brecksville, Cuyahoga County, Calvin farmed with his father and brothers his entire life. He married Susanna Campbell, of Canada East, on 25 Feb 1841. The 1850 census finds him working as a farm laborer in Saybrook Township, Ashtabula County, OH. By 1860, Calvin, wife Susanna, and children; Emily (b. 1841), Almeda (b. 1843), and William (b. 1856), are farming and living in Independence Township, Cuyahoga County, OH. During the next decade Calvin moved to Paulding County where he purchased 40 acres on 23 Nov 1877. He died the following 16 July 1878, and is buried in Prairie Chapel Cemetery, Oakwood, Brown, Paulding, Ohio (east side of the road, Row 2 (find a grave memorial #37891549).

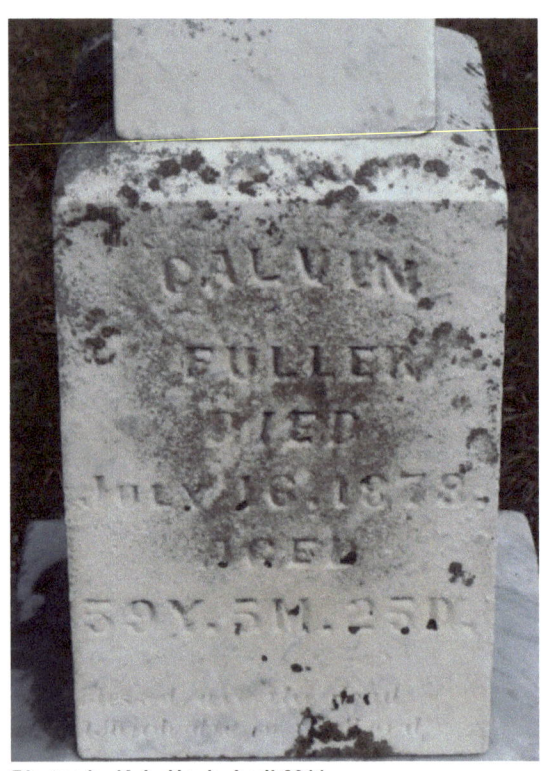

Photos by K. L. Houk, April 2011

## ORPHELIA FULLER BELDEN (1823 – 1865)

Lola Partain of Muldrow, Oklahoma has provided much of the information we have on Orphelia Fuller. Born in Brecksville, Cuyahoga, Ohio in 1823, Orphelia was married to Jabez Devatus (Joe Belden), a farmer from Massachusettes, on 4 Apr 1839. The couple lived near Jacob and Lucy initially and later moved to Chemung Township, McHenry, Illinois. In 1960, they are shown in census records as farming and residing in Grayson, Texas. Their children were as follow: Isahel Albert Goodrich Beldon (1843-1886); Cornelia Beldon (b. in 1844); Alfred M. Beldon (b. in 1847); Henry Andrew Beldon (b. in 1848); Willis Belden (b. in 1851); Phoebe Roxanne Belden (1853-1920; Charles Beldon (b. in 1855); and Anna (Annie) Martha Beldon (1861-1884). Orphelia died shortly after the birth of her 8th child. Her husband remarried on 25 Sep 1863 and the family moved once again to Missouri.

Above: 1st Grayson County, TX Courthouse, 1846

East side of Courthouse Square, Sherman, Grayson, 1868 (Photos: Grayson County website)

## WILLIS FULLER (1828 – Aft. 1880)

Willis Fuller was also born in Brecksville, Cuyahoga Co., OH, but never married. He farmed with his brother Calvin throughout his life. After Calvin's death, Willis continued to farm his land and lived with Calvin's widow, Susan, in Perry Township, Putnam Co., Ohio. (1880 census) He had no children.

Bogart Cemetery, Putnam County, Ohio (Photo by K. L. Houk, April 2011)

## CYNTHIA FULLER ELLIOTT (1834 - aft 1900)

Cynthia A. Fuller was born to Jacob and Mary Eldridge Cole in Brecksville, Cuyahoga County, OH in 1834. She was living with her parents in Sept. 1850 when the census was taken, but was living with her husband James Asbury Elliott, farm laborer, either with her parents or next to them in August 1860, in Pleasant Township, Putnam County, Ohio. The couple had five children: Mary Elliott (b. in 1863); John J. Elliott (b. in 1864); Charles F. Elliott (b. in 1866); James A. Elliott (b. in 1867); and Harriet Elliott (b. in 1873). They lived in Columbus Grove, Putnam Co until after 1900.

In 1859 The Baltimore and Ohio Railroad became the first railroad to run through Columbus Grove. In 1902 the addition of a streetcar service that ran into Lima was established. (Photo: K. L. Houk)

## MARIA FULLER (1837 - Unknown)

The second daughter of Jacob Fuller and Mary Eldridge Cole, Maria was 13 and living with her parents in Brecksville, Cuyahoga County, OH, at the time of the 1850 census. Her married name is not known at the present time and it is possible she did not move with the family to Putnam County.

## JACOB E. FULLER (1838 - TBD )

Jacob E. Fuller was born to Jacob Fuller and Mary Eldridge Cole in 1838 in Brecksville, Cuyahoga County, OH and moved with the family to Putnam County. He served with the Third Ohio Veteran Volunteer Cavalry from 4 Sep 1861 to 4 Aug 1865 during the Civil War. On 11 Dec 1866, Jacob married Frances M. Greene and they lived in Columbus Grove, Pleasant Township, Putnam County with Jacob Senior following the death of Mary Eldridge Cole. The 1870 census shows them living with Jacob W. Fuller (son of Matthew Fuller), his wife Mallisa and daughters Elizabeth and Viola. Jacob E. and Frances had two daughters (Mary, age 2 and Fanny M., infant) who were given up for adoption after the death of their mother in 1871. (Probate files on record at Putnam County Court House). Mary was adopted by Henry Ayers and his wife. Fanny M. was adopted by A. R. Vandoren and his wife. Both couples lived in Putnam County, OH.

Presbyterian Church, Columbus Grove, Pleasant Township, Putnam County, Ohio (Photo: April, 2011 by K. L. Houk)

Know all men by these presents
That I Jacob E Fuller of the County
of Douglas and State of Kansas. do
hereby give my full Consent and do
fully authorize A. R. Vandoren & wife
of the County of Putnam and State of Ohio
to take possession of and assume Control of
my Child Fanny M. Fuller an infant and
adopt her as their own Child and I
do hereby resign unto the Said Vandoren & wife
all acthority and Control vested in me
as her natural father and guardian
This Consent is given with the assurance
from the Said Vandoren & Wife that
they will be unto Said Child a father
and Mother and in love and affection
treat her as a daughter and make
Suitable provision for her physical moral
and Mental welfare during the years of
her Minority and that the relation of
this Child Shall be unto them the Said
Vandoren & Wife the Same in law
and fact as if born unto them as
their own
   Witness my hand and Seal
this 4th day July 1871
Attest                    Jacob Fuller
L F Green                           {Seal}

Know all men by these presents

That I Jacob E Fuller of the County of Douglas and State of Kansas do hereby give my full Consent and do fully authorize Henry Ayers and wife of the County of Putnam and State of Ohio to take possession and assume Control of My Child Mary Fuller and adopt her as their own and I do hereby resign unto them all authority and Control over said Child now vested in me by virtue of being her natural Father and guardian

This consent is given with the assurance from Henry Ayers and wife that they will be unto this Child a Father and Mother and in love and affection treat her as a daughter & provide for her Physical Moral and Mental Culture during the years of her minority and that her relation to the said Henry Ayers and wife shall be the same in Law and fact as if born unto them as their own now & henceforth

Witness My hand and Seal This 4th day of July 1871

Attest
L. F. Green

Jacob E Fuller [Seal]

## HARRY T FULLER, REV. (1840-1928)

Photo: K. L. Houk

Of all the Fuller children, Harry has the most varied resume and the only reference to a spiritual commitment. Farming was his primary occupation, but Harry was also an ordained minister in the Church of the United Brethren and served as a Corporal in Company I, Ohio 88th Infantry Regiment from 30 July 1863 to 3 July 1865 during the Civil War. Harry married Polly Carnahan on 6 Nov 1869 in Putnam County.

Harry and Polly had six children, not all living to adulthood. Surviving children were Samuel Montgomery Fuller (1875-1971) and James Fuller (1890-1927). The Fullers also raised Minnie Miller, Opha D. Carnahan, and Nellie M. Carnahan. Also living with them in the 1910 census; Lilly M. Fuller, born 1892; and Riley E. Fuller, born 1909.

---

FULLER, RILEY ELLIS

Son of James Edward and Lily Mae (Mumea) Fuller was born in Paulding County, OH, Feb. 21, 1909. He was a veteran of W.W. II. His death was Nov. 25, 1963. He never married. Burial was in the Prairie Chapel Cemetery near Oakwood, OH, Lot No. 67, West Side.

---

(Retyped Obituary for grandson Riley Ellis Fuller)

## Obituary
### POLLY FULLER

Polly Fuller daughter of James and Lucinda Carnahan, was born June 27, 1850 at Olivesburg, Ohio. When but a year old she came with her parents to Oakwood, in which vicinity she spent the remainder of her long life. She was the second oldest of twelve children and the last survivor. Passing from this life, at the home of her son, Sam Fuller December 31, 1945.

She was married to Harry Fuller, November 7, 1869. To this union five children were born, four of them preceded her in death, two in infancy and Lucinda and James. Sam Fuller, of Oakwood, with whom she made her home the past few years. Her husband preceded her in death on December 27, 1923.

She also took into her home and raised as her own daughters, Mrs. Minnie Sheeley of La Verne, California, Mrs. Orpha Titler and Nellie Winchester, both of Adrian, Michigan.

There are seven grandchildren and ten great grandchildren many other relatives and a host of friends.

Funeral services were held in the Church of the Brethren, at Dupont. The Rev. David Landis, pastor officiating. Interment was made in the Prairie Chapel Cemetery, where her husband was also buried.

---

FULLER SAMUEL M.

Son of Rev. Harry and and Polly (Carnahan) Fuller was born near Beckersville Ohio April 7, 1875 and departed this life near Oakwood Ohio A Aug. 21, 1970 in Mandale, Paulding County Ohio. He and his family moved near Oakwood Ohio when he was 2 years of age and settled on a farm. In his youth he went to Michigan to work in a stave mill for a few years. Oct. 12, 1901 he married Anna Peal Woggerman of Oakwood Ohio. to this union was born a daughter, Mrs Clifford ( Gertrude) Keck RED 1 Oakwood Ohio; two sons Kenneth of Scotsdale Ariz,: and Harry , deceased of Oakwood Ohio. They remained in Michigan for two years ahd then returned to Oakwood where they operated a hardwarebuisness for a period time. Most of His active time he worked as a painter, carpenter, and paped hanger. im 1913 he went to Galveston Tex. to help in the rebuilding of houses after a tidal wavestruck. later he came back to Ohio and worked in airplane factory in Troy Ohio after the World War ll. Other survisorsare a dauther-in-law Mrs. Marie Fuller, a foster sister Orphia Titler of Sand Creek Mich,; 9 gtand children; 15 great grand-children and many other relatives.Preceeding him in death was his wife, Anna; son harry; brother james; a sister Cindy and two foster sisters; MinnieSheeley and Nellie ( Carnahan)Onstead Burial was in Little Auglaize Cemetary near Melrose ohio lot No. 2-32 West side

## Section 2: ABEL B. FULLER'S STORY

Jacob's eldest son, Abel B. Fuller, was born in New York 2 July 1805, probably in Washington County near Whitehall. He came to Ohio with his family and married Roxana Cole (assumed to be the daughter of neighbor Warren Cole). The young couple bought 50 acres from Jacob in 1833 in Brecksville, Cuyahoga Co., but sold it prior to their move to what would be Pleasant Township, Putnam County, Ohio.

Unlike Brecksville, Pleasant Township had no roads and Abel's 120-acre tract of land was located in the edge of the Black Swamp (see map below). Having obtained the land in 1833 from the Ottawa Indians, the government sold the swamp land for $1.25/acre to attract new settlers to the area and to raise funds to build a series of canals connecting the Ohio River to Lake Erie.

Abel and Roxana would have built and lived in a cabin, "...made of layers of logs, notched to fit one another. The cracks were stopped with mortar of a mixture of clay and straw or grass. The roof was of clapboards, which were held in place by weight poles. The weight poles were held in place by "knees" of hard timber. The floor, doors, tables, and stools were puncherons, logs shaved off on one side in order that a fairly respectable level surface was presented." ("Once Upon A Sugar Grove" Souvenir of the Columbus Grove, Ohio Centennial 1864-1964.)

Typical 1850's cabin, Photo by K. L. Houk

RANGE 7 EAST. TOWNSHIP 1 SOUTH

## MAP OF PLEASANT TOWNSHIP

- 1835, ABEL B. FULLER'S 120-ACRE PARCEL
- 1837, MATTHEW FULLER'S 80-ACRE LAND GRANT

Scale 50 Chains =

*"Because of this swamp condition, ague, typhoid fever, and other maladies were common to the early settlers of Putnam County. Holes were dug in the swampy ground and a portion of the water that seeped in the excavations was used....One of the most difficult jobs was that of removing the large trees so that cultivation could take place. The trees would be girdled and after the foliage had died, vegetables could be planted among the roots of the dead tree. The most common vegetable was the turnip. The tree would then be felled and burned and then the grain crops were planted. The biggest task was to get the grain ground after all other things were overcome. Settlers joined teams together and often drove fifty or sixty miles with their grain in order to reach a grist mill."* (**"Once Upon A Sugar Grove" Souvenir of the Columbus Grove, Ohio Centennial 1864-1964.**)

Abel may have found his acreage too much to handle as he quickly sold a large portion of it. His brother, Matthew, also sold portions of his land to family. Only a sampling of the various deeds remain, due to a flood at the Kalida Courthouse. Abel appears to have been involved in a multi-year legal battle over property (perhaps tax related) that was ruled against him in three successive Sheriff sales, the last in 1853, three years before his death.

Neither could Abel retain a wife. His first wife, Roxana Cole, died in 1840. Second wife, Prudence Rachel Mayberry died in 1846. Catherine Ann Pence, wife #3 (and 22 years his junior) outlived him, remarrying local farmer David Ditzler 3 ½ years after Abel's death.

Abel's real estate holdings were valued at $1,000 in the 1850 census. Following his death in June 1856, his son, Harless C. Fuller, was appointed administrator and guardian of Abel's minor children. Harless found himself defending his father's estate against his third wife, Orson D. and Jonathan Cole Fuller. The issues were finally resolved at a Sheriff's sale on the steps of the County Courthouse in Ottawa on 20 May 1858 when Abel's remaining 40 acres were divided between Orson and his brother Jonathan, the highest bidders at $334. (**Kalida Sentinel, Newspaper Notices compiled by Marguerite Crist Calvin, 1855-1860**) Abel's debts came to $101.32 (**record on file at Putnam Courthouse**); mostly for services and supplies rendered to him by Harless.

As with Jacob Fuller, Sr., Mary Cole, and other members of the family, no record of Abel's birth, death or burial has been found as of 1 October 2011. It is possible a small family plot was used. All but one of his children appear to have lived out their lives in Ohio.

ABEL FULLER          P. 199

Abel Fuller son of Jacob and            Fuller IN an
Eastern state. Married Sept 6,1828 to Roxana Cole, first
marriage. To this union were born five children as follows;
Orson D born July 30,1829 died 1899, Sarah Ann
born Oct 10     1831 ( No date of death known), Infant
daughter born Apr 19,1833, Hanless, born June 23, 1834 (
no date of death shown,0 and Conantha C born Sept 23,1837
died Oct 28,1905.
Abel's second marriage to
Prudence Mayberry born Nov 29,1807 died Oct 20, 1846
Children are as follow ; William born June 15,1841 died Aug 1,1
1841, Losia ( Fuller) Timbers born Apr 28,1842 died Nov 30,
1909, Nancy Elizabeth born May 26,1943 ( no date of death
shown). Lucy Fuller Born Aug 4,1845, ( No date of death shown)
Jacob Fuller Born Oct 4, 1846 .( No date of death shown).
Jesse E born July 20, 1837 , ( Np date of death shown,also
doubt the corect date of birth ).
Abels third marriage was Apr 11,1847 to Kathryn Ann Pence
born Oct 4,1827. Children are as follows.: nfant son born
Oct 29,1848 died Nov 19, 1848 1848, Maryellen born June 6,1850.
( no date of death shown), Phoebe Roxanna born Apr 24,1853 (
no date of death shown)., Abel B born Jany 11,1856 died May
17, 1856

(Note: The above obituary, which appears to be a draft, was obtained from the Putnam County Historical Society. No other public obituary was located. K. L. Houk)

Photo by K. L. Houk

Abel Fuller's life appears to have been lived in difficult circumstances (supplies in Columbus Grove were bought with animal furs because money was so scarce) which perhaps shortened his tenure. Five of his 15 children did not reach adolescence. Historical statistics cannot give insight into a person's temperament, intelligence, or world view. His early death, numerous court cases, and multiple land dealings do raise questions as to his personality and state of health. We are left to ponder.

## ABEL FULLER'S CHILDREN

| Name | Occupation | HH/ Estate Value | Spouse | Children | Residence | Death & Burial |
|---|---|---|---|---|---|---|
| Orson D. Fuller | Blacksmith | $4,000 | 1. Ellen Mayberry   2. Mary Jamison  3. Cynthia Jamison | 6 | Putnam Co, OH | 28 Sep. 1899 |
| Sarah Ann Fuller | Homemaker | $500 | William P. Bowers Farmer | 2 | Pleasant, Putnam Co, OH | 12 July 1852, Putnam Co. OH |
| Harless C. Fuller | Laborer | $400 | Mary E. Farnum | 5 | Pleasant & Henry Co, OH | Before 1880 |
| Jonathan Cole Fuller | Laborer, Carpenter, Farmer | N/A | Martha Smith | 12 | Putnam Co, OH, KS & OK | 16 Nov 1905, Fairview Cemetery Woods Co, OK |
| Louise Fuller | Homemaker | N/A | Theodore A. Timbers, Laborer | 7 | Putnam & Paulding Co, OH | 30 Nov 1909 Prairie Chapel Cemetery Putnam Co, OH |
| Nancy Elizabeth Fuller | Homemaker | N/A | Miles Barfell | 5 | Putnam Co, OH | 25 Nov 1873 Putnam Co, OH |
| Lucy Ann Fuller | Homemaker | N/A | Thomas Irvin Louthan | 8 | Putnam Co, OH | 9 Dec 1917 Putnam Co, OH |
| Jacob Fuller | Day Laborer | N/A | Isabelle Hubble | 6 | Putnam Co, OH | 24 July 1928 Truro Cemetery Putnam Co., OH |
| Mary Ellen Fuller | Homemaker | N/A | Johnson M. Smith, Farmer | 9 | Putnam Co, OH | 8 Nov 1933, Putnam Co., OH |
| Phoebe Roxana Fuller | Homemaker | N/A | James Bracy Laborer, Stone Quarry | 7 | Putnam Co, OH | 15 Mar 1923, Putnam Co, OH |
|  |  |  |  |  |  | Chart by K.L. Houk |

Note: Five of Abel's 15 childen did not survive to adolescence: Infant daughter (1833), William (1841), Jesse E. (1847), Infant son (1848), and Abel B. (1856).

## ORASON DELBERT FULLER

Abel's eldest son was perhaps the most successful and outgoing of his children. Born in Brecksville in 1829, Orson D. Fuller moved with his parents to Putnam County, By the time he was 21, Columnist Imogene Elwer, in *"Chronicles of the Past"* tells us, *"O.D. Fuller had a blacksmith shop located immediately behind the courthouse,"* in 1850. He is listed as a blacksmith in the Business Directory of the Kalida Sentinel (Vol. 1, #28) on 11 Sep 1855, but dissolved his Blacksmithing partnership with A. Stemmons 31 Aug 1858 and closed his business two years later; *"Take Notice – I would inform my old friends and patrons that I am closing up my business in this place and that I am in debt and must pay up and to do so, I am forced to ask for what is due me.---those indebted to me personally or firm of Fuller & Slemmons to call and pay up.---"Rememer well, and bear in mind; Your broke up friend is not hard to find." O(ut of) D(ollars) Fuller."* Kalida, February 23, 1860.

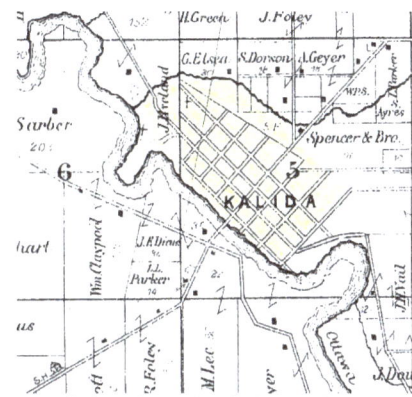

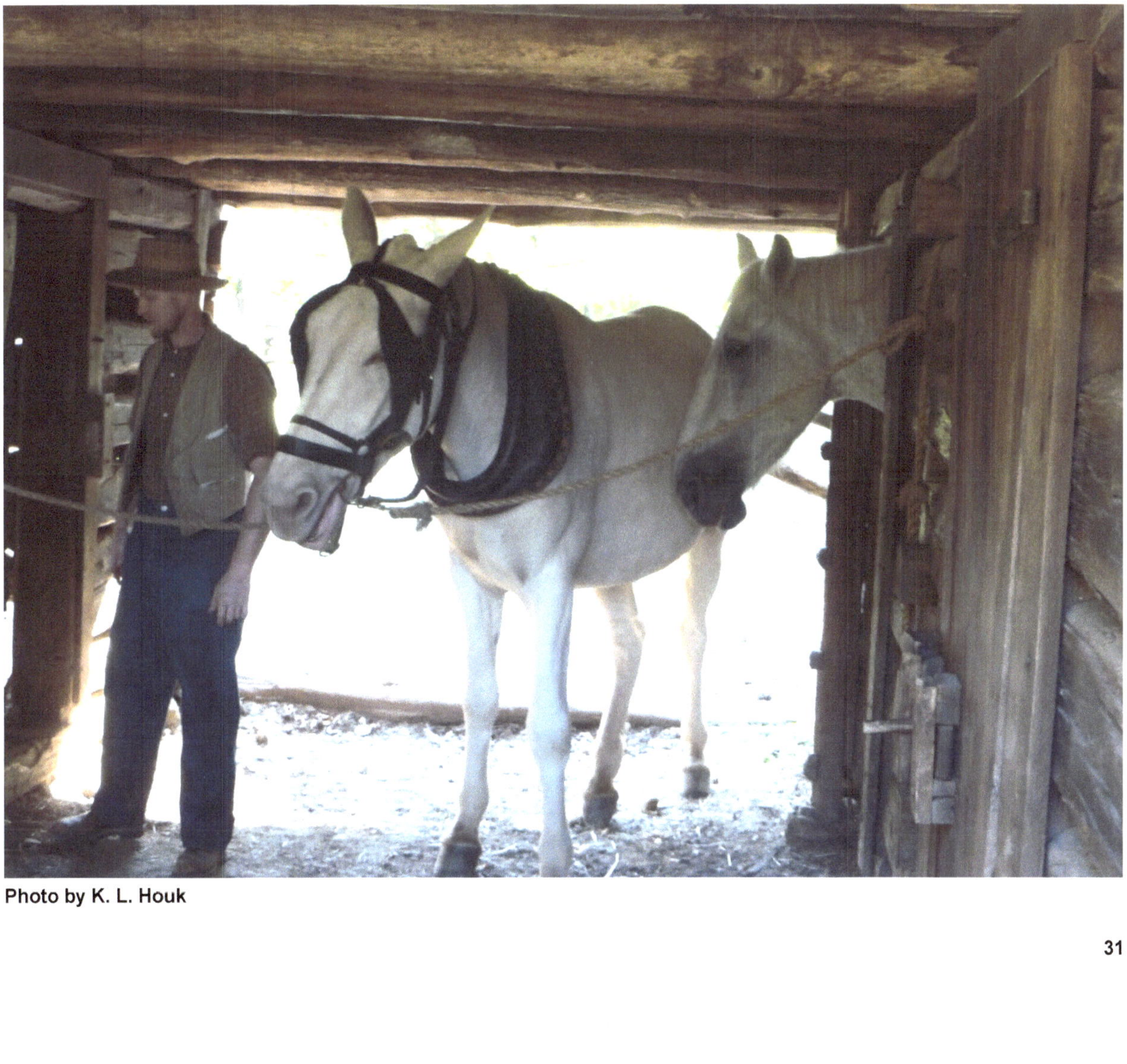

Photo by K. L. Houk

It is not hard to imagine why Orson was in debt. He had been appointed guardian of Abel's minor children (Louisa, Nancy Elizabeth, Jacob, Mary Ellen, and Phebe) after Abel's death in 1856. The Historical Hand Atlas of Paulding County, Ohio 1882, provides more family details.

*"ORSON D. FULLER—was born in Cuyahoga county, Ohio, July 30, 1829. His parents were Able B. and Roxanna (Cole) Fuller, both died in Putnam county, Ohio; the former in June, 1856, the latter in April, 1840. He has been thrice married. His first wife was Ellen, daughter of James and Mary Mayberry and to whom one child was born, Nancy M., July 14, 1852: She lives in Brown township. His second wife was Mary Jamison, a sister of his present wife; he has two children by this wife, John Francis, born August 27, 1854; Alexander T., December 13, 1857; both reside in Brown township. The present Mrs. Fuller is Cynthia, daughter of Francis and Rachel (Wroten) Jamison, both of whom are deceased—the father in Putnam county and the mother in Allen county. She was born in Allen county, Ohio, October 27, 1833, and their marriage took place in Putnam county, Ohio, March 4, 1860. They have three children: Mary A. born 1862; Julia E., April 7, 1864; Rachel F., August 25, 1866, died November 29, 1878. Mr. Fuller has no less than five different families residing under his roof, among whom there has always been a harmonius feeling (emphasis added). He has been Clerk of the Courts in this county for three years. He had two brothers, Jonathan and Jacob, in the war of 1861; the first was a member of the 57th Ohio. Orson is a farmer and a blacksmith. He settled in this county in November, 1865. Address, Oakwood, Paulding county, Ohio."*

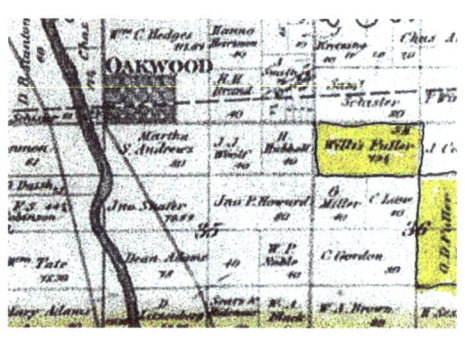

Orson D. and Cynthia Fuller's tombstone is located in the Prairie Chapel Cemetery, Brown Township, Paulding County, Ohio. The inscription reads:

**ORSON D. FULLER**
**DIED SEP 28, 1899**
**AGED 70 Y. 1 M. 28 D.**

**CINTHA, HIS WIFE**
**DIED APR. 19, 1900**
**AGED 68 Y. 6 M. 22 D.**

## SARAH ANN FULLER

Few records have been located to document the life of Sarah Ann Fuller, Abel's eldest daughter. She was married at age 15 to William P. Bowers, a blacksmith (perhaps an acquaintance of her brother, Orson). They were married on 4 Nov 1846. Bowers was 21 years older than Sarah. The couple had two children, Elizabeth Ellen (1848-1864) and Abel Fuller Bowers (1850- ?). They were living in Pleasant Township, Putnam County, Ohio in 1850. The marriage ended prior to William's marriage to Hannah Marole on 14 Apr 1853. In 1860, the two children are living with Solomon and Susanna Schlosser in Putnam County, Ohio. Sarah is found again in the 1880 census, living with her son, Abel Fuller Bowers, I Jackson Township, Hardin, Ohio, where the son is a laborer.

## HARLESS C. FULLER

Abel's second son, Harless C. Fuller, was born in Brecksville, and moved with his parents to Putnam County. He was the executor of his father's will (1856-1858) and caught in the family dynamics contesting the settlement of Abel's estate. Harless married Mary E. Farnam on 11 Nov 1860. The couple had five children; Charles (b. 1861), Samuel (b. 1864), Alvada (b. 1866), Alvira (b. 1867), and Manon (b. 1869). They had moved to Washington Township, Henry County, OH by the 1870 census which shows Harless's occupation as that of day laborer. By the 1880 census, the family is no longer intact. Samuel Miles (16) is working on the farm of Robert W. Dennis, and records have not been found for the remainder. It is possible the younger daughters may have been adopted.

## JONATHAN COLE FULLER

Jonathan will be discussed in depth in the next section of this book. He was born in Putnam County, 29 Sep 1837, and was the last child of Abel B. Fuller and Roxanna Cole.

## LOUISA FULLER

The second child of Abel B. Fuller and Prudence Rachel Mayberry, Louisa was born in Columbus Grove, Putnam County, Ohio on 28 Apr 1842. She married Theodore A. Timbers, a day laborer on 10 April 1862 in Putnam County. The couple had seven children; William (b. 1861), Theany (1864-1929), Elizabeth (b. 1865), Rosetta (b. 1868), Jessie A. (1876-1908), and Eddie E. Timbers (b. 1884). By 1900, her husband had bought a farm near Oakwood, in Paulding County and four of her seven children were still living. Louisa died on 30 Nov 1909 and is buried in Prairie Chapel Cemetery.

## NANCY ELIZABETH FULLER

Born to Abel B. Fuller and Prudence Rachel Mayberry on 28 May 1843 in Columbus Grove, Putnam County, OH.; Nancy E. lived her life in the same area. At age 16, she married Miles Barfell, Day Laborer, on 15 May 1860, and bore him six children: Louisa (b.1861), Mary Ellen (1862-1887), Thomas (b. 1864), William (b. 1868), Isadore (b. abt 1870), and Miles Leroy Barfell (1873-1934). Her husband apparently died between the 1870 and 1880 census. In 1880, Nancy is found married to local farmer George W. Murray. George died prior to the 1910 census which shows Nancy as a widow living in Pleasant Township, Putnam County, OH. From state death records, it is estimated she died on 12 Feb 1913.

## LUCY ANN FULLER

Columbus Grove was the birthplace of Lucy Ann Fuller, born 4 Aug 1845 to Abel and Prudence Fuller. By age 15, Lucy was working as a nanny for the children of John S. Gander, a local farmer, and his wife, Elizabeth. She married Thomas Irvin Louthan, a day laborer, on 16 Jan 1862, when she was 16. The 1900 census shows only four of Lucy's eight children were still living. The eight children's names were: John M. (b. 1863), Marietta J. (b. 1865), Jesse B. (b. 1867), George B. (1871-1960), Mary E. (1874-1876), Lizzie C. (b. 1878), Orson R. (b. 1880), and Adolpha Brooks (1883-1980). The couple lived in Sugar Creek Township, Putnam County, OH until their deaths. Lucy died 9 Dec 1917. Her death was attributed to arterial sclerosis.

## JACOB FULLER

Jacob Fuller (4 Oct 1846 – 24 Jul 1928) was Abel's youngest living son. As was common with large families, he was "farmed out" at age 14, as a laborer on the farm of Robert and Henrietta Jamison (probably relatives of Orson D. Fuller's wife), and lived adjacent to his older brother. Jacob joined the 88th Regiment of the Ohio Volunteer Infantry during the Civil War and served two years (1863-1865). Like his older brother Jonathan, he came home from the war with chronic diarrhea which prevented him from holding full-time work for the balance of his life.

Jacob married Isabell Hubble (13 Aug 1869) and the couple had six children, four of whom were living in 1900: Thomas (b. 1871), Grace (b. 1879), Edward Eugene (b. 1882), and Homer J. (b. 1889). Foster daughter Ima F. Fuller was also living with them in 1910.

In his later years, Jacob was accused of being incompetent, however the Probate Judge, in 1925, ordered his son Edward to care for him, with routine supervisory visits from County officials. Jacob died 24 July 1928 and is buried in Truro Cemetery, Putnam County, Ohio.

---

In the matter of guardianship of Jacob Fuller,
An alleged incompetent

IN THE PROBATE COURT OF PUTNAM COUNTY, OHIO

JOURNAL ENTRY
July 31-1925

This day, this matter came on to be and was heard on the evidence and arguments of the counsel, and the Court being fully advised in the premises, finds that the application filed herein should be and is hereby dismissed.

The Court, further orders that said Jacob Fuller shall remain in the home of Edward Fuller, his son; that said Edward Fuller shall keep the home and the person of Jacob Fuller as clean as can possibly be done under the circumstances, and the physical condition of said Jacob Fuller.

It is further ordered that Jacob Allen, humane officer, shall be permitted to enter the home of said Edward Fuller at all reasonable hours for the purpose of investigation as to the condition of said home and said Jacob Fuller. Case dismissed without record Costs taxed

_____
Probate Judge

---

Lima News
26 July 1928

COLUMBUS GROVE, July 26—Services for Jacob Fuller, 81, Civil war veteran, who died Tuesday night, were held Thursday afternoon at the Christian church. Rev. John A. Stover, the pastor, officiated at the service. Interment was in Truro cemetery southwest of Columbus Grove.

Fuller had been seriously ill, suffering from a complication of diseases and age. His wife died some years ago. He is survived by two sons, Thomas and Edward Fuller, both of Columbus Grove.

## MARY ELLEN FULLER

Mary Ellen was only six when her father, Abel Fuller, died in 1856. She lived with her mother, Catharine Ann, remarried to farmer David Ditzler, when the 1860 Census was taken. The family lived next to Jacob Fuller, Sr., and his wife, Mary. Mary Ellen spent her life in Putnam County, marrying farmer Johnson M. Smith on 8 Dec 1870. The couple had nine children, eight of whom were living in 1910. The children's names were: Olive (b. 1870), John (b. 1872), Elizabeth L. (b. 1874), Myrtle Anna (1876-1963), Harry A. (b. 1878), Frank R. (b. 1880), Emma Bertha (1882-1973), Blaine (b. 1884), and Lorenzo (1887-1889). Mary Ellen died on 8 Nov 1933 in Putnam County, OH.

## PHOEBE ROXANA FULLER

Phoebe Roxana, like Mary Ellen, lived with her mother Catharine Ann Pence Fuller Ditzler in 1860, next to grandfather Jacob, Sr. and grandmother, Mary Cole. She married local farmer James L. Bracy on 26 Aug 1875 in Putnam County. They raised seven children: Edd (1876-1935), George E. (b. 1877), James Harry (1878-1959), John (b. 1883), Aurora Orlin (b. 1886), Rosa (b. 1887), and Ortha H. (1888-1952). They also lived in Riley Township, Putnam County. Phoebe died in Putnam County on 15 Mar 1923.

Abel's generation transformed the Black Swamp into fertile farmland at a high cost. It is hard to comprehend our ancestors drinking milk from cows that had eaten poisonous white snakeroot, causing milk sickness in the 1840s and 1850s, often killing the unsuspecting victim (especially children). **("The Great Black Swamp" by Carolyn V. Platt, TIMELINE, Ohio Historical Society, February-March 1987.)** The next generation would pay an even higher price, transforming two governmental ideologies into one during the Civil War.

# Section 3: JONATHAN COLE FULLER'S STORY

The story of Jonathan Cole Fuller is a sorrowful one. Born to Abel B. and Roxana Fuller on 29 Sep 1837, Jonathan's mother died three years later. He was living with his second step-mother in 1850, (Catharine Ann Pence), and was 18 when his father, Abel B. Fuller, died. According to the Kalida Sentinel, Orson and Jonathan each bid the highest amount ( a little over $300) for Abel's remaining 40 acres of land and split the property, although no deeds were found to confirm this action. Jonathan is not listed in the 1860 census, although later family testimony to the U.S. Army stated that Jonathan lived with Orson both prior to and after his military service.

Photo: From family collection of Stefani Sheddy Ferguson

On 20 June 1861, Jonathan enlisted as a Private in Company F of the 25$^{th}$ Ohio Volunteer Infantry (O.V.I.). He stood 5' 7 ½" tall, with dark complexion, hazel eyes, and dark hair; occupation: farmer - strong, able to chop trees. (We are indebted to Mary Nussbaum for her notes on Jonathan's military career, taken from the National Archives.)

*"Enlisted for three years on 20 June 1861 at Camp Case, Columbus, Ohio, in Company F of the 25$^{th}$ Regiment of the Ohio Voluntary Infantry. Id duty in West Virginia. Action at Cheat Mountain on Sept 12 and Greenbrier River, October 3-4. Expedition to Camp Baldwin, Dec 11-13, 1861. Action at Camp Allegheny, Buffalo Mountain on Dec. 12. Summary: on 13 Dec 1861; 20 killed /mortally wounded; 107 wounded; 10 captured/missing. On the muster roll for the end of Dec. 1861, Jonathan was reported 'killed at the Battle of Baldwin.' A corrected mustser roll for Jan/Feb read that he had been captured, and was a prisoner in Richmond, VA.*

Jonathan was in prison from 24 Dec 1861 to 23 Feb 1862, when he was exchanged. While there, he was reported to have contracted mumps and diarrhea. He was furloughed in March 1862 and returned to live with Orson while being treated by a docter. When partially recovered he returned to his regiment, but was 'absent, sick in Hospital at Cumberland, Md. in May and June of 1862. August found Jonathan sick from "colica" (on the 8$^{th}$); jaundice (on the 16$^{th}$); measles (on the 19$^{th}$); then hospitalized August 27 and September 22 and given a disability discharge from Fairfax Seminary Hospital near Alexandria on 10 Oct 1862 with a diagnosis of 'phithisis pulmonalis'" (i.e. pulmonary consumption).

It was possible Jonathon met his future wife, Martha Jane Smith, through his younger sister, Lucy Ann Fuller. The 1960 census shows both girls working as nannies for the Gander Brothers in Sugar Creek Township, Putnam County. Martha Jane (age 14) was working for Lewis Gander, a local merchant. Lucy Ann (age 15) was working for John S. Gander. Jonathan and Martha were married on 1 Jan 1863 in Putnam County, OH, in the home of Orson D. Fuller, by Reverend Steaman, D.D. and M. D. The couple lived four miles east of Delphos, according to Mary Nussbaum's notes; then during the summer of 1863 they rented a farm northwest of Vaughnsville in Sugar Creek Township, Putnam County. On 4 July 1863, the trustees of the township excepted Jonathan from the draft because of his disability.

# MARRIAGE RECORD.

Winter 1863-64 found Jonathan and Martha moved to Cairo, Allen County, Ohio, where he was a day laborer, finding work wherever he could. It is quite possible economic needs forced him to re-enlist on 2 May 1864 for 100 days with Company C of the 151st O.V.I. He was sent to drill troops on the grand rapids of the Potomac. His regiment saw action at Fort Stevens, on 11 and 12 July 1864; repulsing a confederate attack on Washington, D.C. Abraham Lincoln and his wife Mary were seen observing the battle. On 27 Aug 1864, Jonathan was mustered out with his unit.

**Civil War guns at Fort Stevens, Washington, D.C.**

Fort Stevens was part of the extensive fortifications built around Washington D.C. during the American Civil War. It was constructed in 1861 as "Fort Massachusetts" and later enlarged by the Union Army and renamed "Fort Stevens" after Brig. Gen. Isaac Ingalls Stevens, who was killed at the Battle of Chantilly, Virginia, on 1 Sep 1862.  (Source: Wikipedia)

Jonathan returned from the Civil War to meet his first child, Alice Roxana, born 12 July 1864. Mary Nussbaum's notes again provide first-hand details. *"After he (Jonathan) came home they lived for about a year in Vaughnsville in Putnam County (about nine miles from Cairo). Their second child, Katherine Sevilia, was born there on 24 Nov 1865. In 1866, Jonathan found carpentry work in Pendleton, Putnam County and the family moved yet again to Pendleton where they remained until the spring of 1885 when they went to Kansas.* Katherine died 5 Jan 1867 and is buried in the Pendleton Cemetery. Jonathan's health continued to prevent him from earning a living. During the eight years they lived four miles NE of Pendleton, he received only $1.50 a day, unable to keep up with able-bodied men who earned $2.50 a day for the same work. On July 8, 1879, Jonathan filed for his military pension. By 1883, he was partially bed-ridden, limited to chores and light labor. Their 12$^{th}$ and last child, Nora Abigail was born 9 Sep 1884. Shortly afterwards, they left behind the graves of three children, intending to relocate to Barber County, KS in January 1885. The March 31, 1885 Kansas Census found them living southeast of Attica, Harper Co., Kansas, *"A large family and no means of support."*

**Kansas Census, March 1$^{st}$, 1885**

The decision to homestead in Kansas was a gutsy call for Martha and Jonathan. The Homestead Act, signed into law by President Abraham Lincoln on 20 May 1862, allowed settlers to claim 160 acres of public land. They paid a small filing fee and then had two options for getting title to the land. If they lived on the 160 acres for five continuous years, built a residence and grew crops, they could then file for their deed for the property. The second option was to purchase the land from the government for $1.25 per acres after living on the land for six months, building a home, and starting to grow crops. What may have attracted Jonathan was an 1864 amendment to the law allowing a soldier with two years of service to acquire the land after a one year residency.

Homesteading in Harper Co., Kansas (Photo: Kansas Historical Foundation)

In her deposition made in application for Jonathan's Civil War Pension, Martha wrote the family took a claim in Sept, 1888 that was about 2 miles south and four miles east of the Attica P. O. and store. Jonathan was admitted to the Military Hospital in Leavenworth, KS the following month, on 9 Oct 1888. The family lived on that claim until the opening of the Cherokee Outlet in Sept, 1893. (Source: Mary Nussbaum's notes)

The five years in Kansas must have been difficult. Drought, scarce natural resources, economic down-turns, living in sod homes with dirt floors, burning corn stalks for fuel winter and summer, and waking up on winter mornings in a snow-covered bed (driven through tiny cracks in the roof during the night) were common occurrences in pioneer memoires. Diseases such as diphtheria had to be treated without doctors and often took the lives of children. Crop failures; outlaws (and no law enforcement); and a simple diet of pancakes, meat grease, light bread, mush and milk made life harsh. Occasionally a young jack-rabbit was caught, fried and served with milk gravy

By 1891, Jonathan (age 54) weighed only 118 lbs. Yet, on Aug. 4$^{th}$ of that year he requested a discharge from the hospital and in December, 1893, the family staked their claim in Woods

County, OK, about 2 ½ miles NE of Winchester, according to Mary Nussbaum's notes. The trip from Attica to Winchester was roughly 46 miles, crossing the Kansas state line and ending *"...about 2 ½ miles NE of Winchester (near Alva, OK)."*  Jonathan's land is shown in the SW section of Section 30.  The Kansas state line is at the top of the map.  Also living in Oklahoma in 1893 (not far from the Fullers) according to Mary's notes, was a man by the name of Edward Stanton Watt.

Jonathan's 1st land claim in Oklahoma, SW Quad. Of Section 30, claimed Dec., 1893.

J. C. Fuller Photo: Stephanie Ferguson

Martha wrote in her deposition that she and the children did the farming.  Jonathan's health continued to be too frail for him assist.  He had been admitted to the National Military Home in Leavenworth, Kansas, for treatment on 9 Oct 1888 and was released on his own recognizance on 4 Aug 1891.  He was re-admitted on 20 April 1900 and remained in the hospital until his death on 16 Nov 1905.  At the time of his death, Jonathan's military pension was $17/mo. Their total property assessment fell from $545 in 1905 to $220 in 1906.

# Jonathan C. Fuller

2964

## MILITARY HISTORY.

| Time and Place of each Enlistment. | Rank. | Company and Regiment. | Time and Place of Discharge. | Cause of Discharge. | Kind and Degree of Disability. | When and Where Contracted. |
|---|---|---|---|---|---|---|
| Camp Chase, Ohio June 20, 1861. | Priv. | F 25th Ohio Inf. | Gen. Hosp. Fairfax Semy. Oct. 13, 1862 | Surgeon's Certif. of Disability | | |
| Lima, Ohio May 2, 1864 | Pvt. | C 151st Ohio Nat. Guards | Camp Chase Ohio Aug. 27, 1864 | Expiration of term of service | Chr. Diarrhea (while Prisoner of war) | Richmond Va Jany 15, 1862. |

## DOMESTIC HISTORY. Protestant.

| WHERE BORN. | Age. | Height. | Complexion. | Color of Eyes. | Color of Hair. | OCCUPATION. | Residence Subsequent to Discharge. | Married or Single. | P. O. Address of Nearest Relative. |
|---|---|---|---|---|---|---|---|---|---|
| Ohio | 50 | 5'7" | Dark | grey | dark | Carpenter | Aetna, Kansas | Married | Martha Jane Fuller Aetna Ks |

## HOME HISTORY.

| Rate of Pension. | Date of Admission and Re-Admission. | Condition of Re-Admission. | Date of Discharge. | Cause of Discharge. | Date of Death. | Cause of Death. |
|---|---|---|---|---|---|---|
| $8. 12.00 $17.00 | Oct. 9, 1888. W.B. R.ad Apr 20, 1900 W.B. | | August 4, 1891 Feb 7, 1906 | At request S.O. 28. Drop'd S.O.8 | | |

## GENERAL REMARKS.

Indebted for clothing 18.45

PAPERS.

Admission Paper, one,
Army Discharge, two,
Certificate of Service, 274 424
Pension Certificate,

Jonathan Fuller is buried in Fairview Cemetery (LAT 365821N & LONG 0984118W). It is located three miles south of Hardtner, KS on US Highway 281, then two miles west. From Alva, it is 11 miles north on U.S. 281, then 2 miles west. Stefani (Schubert) Ferguson, great-great-great-great grand daughter of Jacob Fuller (1785-1872) decorates his grave each Memorial Day. She was born in Medicine Lodge, KS and now lives in Broken Arrow, OK. Stefani has contributed many of the Oklahoma photos in this book, including Jonathan's tombstone (right).

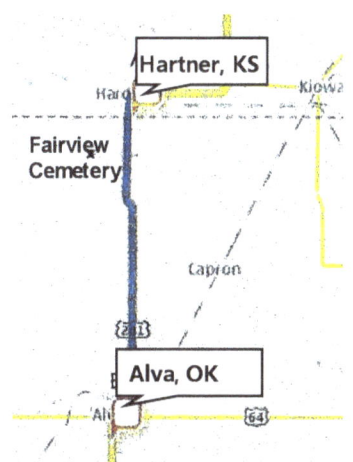

Martha Jane Smith

Martha filed for her widow's pension on 16 Dec 1905. Her widow's pension in 1906 was $8/mo; increased in 1916 to $20/mo; increased in 1926 to $50/mo. She and the children continued to farm their tract and acquired additional land as they could. Martha's address in December, 1907 was P. O. Fitzlen, Woods County, OK. Throughout her almost 37-year marriage, Martha held the family together.

It is here we have an indication of the spiritual beliefs of the Fuller family. Martha Jane Smith, first came to her faith as a member of the United Brethren, in Putnam Co., OH. Perhaps she went to the church served by the Rev. Harry Fuller, son of Jacob Fuller (1785-1872). Martha passed away on 26 Dec 1928 in Morrison, OK. The funeral service was held at the Methodist church in Morrison, conducted by Rev. Demaree of Glencoe, with burial in the Morrison Cemetery. Her obituary reads as follows.

*Martha Jane (Smith) Fuller was born 23 July 1845 in Allen County, Ohio and passed away at her home in Morrison, 26 Dec 1928 at the age of 83 years, 5 months and 3 days. She was married to Jonathan C. Fuller who preceded her in death November 1905 in Alva, Oklahoma. To this union were born twelve children, three girls and three boys still living: Mrs. Sneary of Driftwood, Oklahoma; Joe Fuller of Buffalo, Kansas; Mrs. (Sarah Fuller) Watt of Ellsinore, Missouri; Charles Fuller of Morrison; Mrs. Rogers of Morrison and Virgil Fuller of Kiowa, Kansas, all of whom were present, together with 30 grandchildren and 24 great-grand-children. She confessed her faith in her Savior early in life and united with the United Brethren Church later joining the Methodist by letter.*

*From Ohio she came west with her husband and family in January 1885, and settled in Barber County, Kansas, going through the hardships of those early years. The family came to Oklahoma at the opening of the Cherokee Outlet (16 Sept 1893) and settled near Alva, Oklahoma.*

About twelve years ago Mrs. Fuller came to Morrison and tho advanced in years, maintained her own household. She was a great lover of young people and never missed an opportunity to point out the way to Righteousness. Having an extraordinarily young and active mind for one of her years, she never rested until an obligation *was met, be it a matter of some importance or the recompense to some child for an errand. She had often expressed her desire to go on to Eternal rest, and with her passing comes her reward for faithful service. The hymns she loved best were rendered: "Jesus Lover of My Soul", "Rock of Ages" and "The City Four Square". The scriptural lessons were taken from Rev. 21:1-8, and Hebrews 13 to 14.*

*Card of Thanks: We wish to thank those who assisted us during the sickness and death of our dear mother, also for the beautiful flowers. The Fuller children.*

Rev. 21:1-8

Then I saw a new heaven and a new earth, for the first heaven and the first earth had passed away, and the sea existed no longer. I also saw the Holy City, new Jerusalem, coming down out of heaven from God, prepared like a bride adorned for her husband. Then I heard a loud voice from the throne:

> Look! God's dwelling is with men, and He will live with them. They will be His People and God Himself will be with them and be their God. He will wipe away every tear from their eyes. Death will exist no longer; grief, crying, and pain will exist no longer, because the previous things have passed away.

Then the One seated on the throne said, "Look! I am making everything new." He also said, "Write, because these words are faithful and true." And He said to me, "It is done! I am the Alpha and

The Omega, the Beginning and the End. I will give to the thirsty from the spring of living water as a gift. The victor will inherit these things, and I will be his God, and he will be My son. But the cowards, unbelievers, vile, murderers, sexually immoral, sorcerers, idolaters and all liars – their share will be in the lake that burns with fire and sulfur, which is the second death."

## JONATHAN COLE FULLER'S CHILDREN

| Name | Occupation | Spouse | Children | Residence | Death & Burial |
|---|---|---|---|---|---|
| Alice Roxana | Homemaker | S. E. Bogguss | unknown | Ohio, & Medicine Lodge KS | 20 June 1891 |
| Katherine Sevilla | Daughter | N/A | N/A | Putnam Co, OH | 5 Jan 1867 |
| Thomas Benton | Son | N/A | N/A | Putnam Co., OH | 9 Nov 1878 |
| William Benjamin | Waterworks Engineer | Esther Annie Brooks | 2 | Putnam, Co, OH & Galena, KS | 2 Sep 1906 Galena, KS |
| Elizabeth Alberta | Homemaker | Joseph Prior Sneary | 2 | Putnam Co, OH Barber Co, KS Woods Co, OK | 13 July 1956 Oklahoma City, OK |
| Joseph Clenton (Clinton) | Blacksmith & Wagon Maker | Edith Myrtle Cline | 6 | Putnam Co, OH Barber Co, KS Woodson Co, KS | 8 Aug 1953 Hardtner, KS |
| Sarah Elizabeth | | Edward Stanton Watt | 8 | Missouri | 22 Mar 1956 Poplar Bluff, MO |
| Mary Anna | Daughter | N/A | 0 | Pendleton, Putnam Co, OH | 10 Jan 1877 Putnam Co., OH |
| Charles Leroy | Farmer | Sarah Rebecca Lowden | 12 | Putnam Co, OH KS, MO, OK | 1964 OK |
| Martha J "Mattie" | Homemaker | Mr. Isaac Floyd H. Rogers | 1 1 | Putnam Co, OH Fritzlen Woods, OK | 1946 Morrison, Noble Co, OK |
| John Virgil | Santa Fe RR | Margaret Abigail | 5 | Kiowa, Barber, KS | After 1967 Emporia, KS |
| Nora Abigail | Homemaker | Floyd Adelbert Merryman | None found | Putnam Co., OH KS, OK | 24 Oct 1918 Morrison, OK |
| | | | | | Chart by K.L.Houk |

Three of Jonathan's children did not live to make the trip to Kansas:
Thomas Benton, Mary Ann, and Katherine Sevillia.

## ALICE ROXANA FULLER

Jonathan and Mary's first child, Alice Roxana Fuller, was born in Putnam Co., OH on 12 July 1864. She is shown living with the family in Putnam Co. for the 1880 census, but is not with them in the 1885 census. Her husband (from family records) appears to be S. E. Bogguss, a farmer in Medicine Lodge, KS, but her name is not registered with his on that census. Her death, again from family records, is given as 20 June 1891 in Medicine Lodge, KS.

William Benjamin Fuller

Born in Pendleton, Putnam Co., OH on 18 Dec 1867, William B. Fuller moved to Kansas with his parents and is shown in the 1885 census. He left farming after marrying Ms. Esther Annie Brooks, becoming an engineer in the water works of Galena, KS. It is believed the couple had two children prior to William's early demise. (see story below)

**Esther and William B. Fuller, Galena, KS**

From the Galena, Kansas News: Sept 1906

*William Fuller was seriously wounded by J. A. Luke. Yesterday afternoon about 3 o'clock Wm. Fuller and J.A. Luke, who are employed as engineers at the water works pump house, became engaged in a quarrel, as the result of which Fuller lies in a precarious condition with a bullet in his stomach. Fuller came to town yesterday morning and reported to S.N. Dwight, owner of the water works that Luke was not doing his work properly. When he returned to the pump house, which is located about two miles south of town, he and Luke got into an altercation and he told the latter his conversation with Dwight. At this point Fuller became much enraged and picking up a gas pipe dealt Luke a blow on the head. Luke ran to his house near by and procuring a revolver returned to the pump house where he met Fuller coming towards him still armed with the gas pipe. When the two men were close together Fuller raised the pipe and Luke fired, the ball entering Fuller's stomach. Dr. Payne was summoned, but failed to find the bullet. Fuller is in a serious condition and his recovery is doubtful.* (William Benjamin Fuller died Sep 2, 1906).

## ELIZABETH ALBERTA FULLER

Born on 17 Sep 1871 in Pendleton, OH, Elizabeth Alberta was found in the 1885 Kansas Census living with her family in Harper County. She married Joseph Prior Sneary, a general farmer, in Hazelton, Barber Co., KS on 17 Nov 1895. The couple had two daughters (Gladys, b. 1897, and Grace, b. 1898). They moved to Woods County, Oklahoma where they are shown in each census through 1930. Elizabeth died in Oklahoma City at the age of 84 on 13 July 1956.

# Joseph Clenton (Clinton) Fuller

Joseph Clenton Fuller (born 23 Apr 1873 in Pendleton, OH) was 11 and helping with the family farm in March, 1885, in Harper County, KS. He married Edith Myrtle Cline in 1898 and moved to Barber County, KS where he had a Blacksmith and Wagon shop in Kiowa. By 1920, Joseph owned a farm in Aetna, Barber County, KS and 10 years later was farming in Belmont, Woodson Co, KS. Joseph was the great-great grandfather of Stefani Schubert Ferguson who provided the photo at right.

Photos of Joseph Clenton Fuller family (shared by Stefani Schubert Ferguson)

Joseph and wife, Edyth Myrtle Cline

The Blacksmith Shop

50th Wedding Anniversary
Joseph Fuller & Edith Myrtle Cline

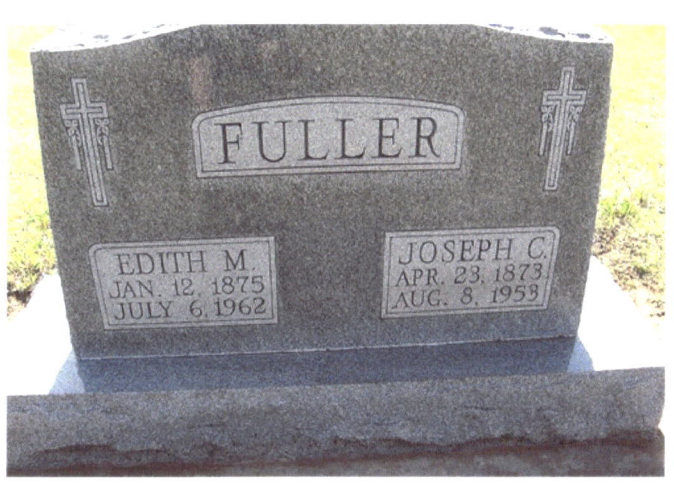

Hardtner Cemetery
Hardtner, KS

Joseph and Edith had the following children; Olean Theadore Fuller (1898-1985), Alma Royal Fuller (1900-1995), Robert Fuller (1903-1903), Verne Doyle Fuller (b. 23 Dec 1904), Harold Earl Fuller (11907-1991) and Helen Fuller (b. 9 June 1909).

## SARAH ELIZABETH FULLER

The 7th child of Jonathan Cole Fuller and Martha Jane Smith; Sarah Elizabeth Fuller, born July 16, 1874, will be discussed more fully in the next section of this document, Section 4.

## CHARLES LEROY FULLER

The epitome of a successful general farmer, Charles Leroy Fuller was born 29 Nov 1877 to Jonathan Cole and Martha Jane Smith and made the journey to Kansas with his parents. He married Sarah Rebecca Lowden in 1901 and they had 12 children. His W.W.I draft registration card gives his height and weight as "Medium." His eyes are blue and his hair is black. Unlike his many of his Fuller ancestors, Charles LeRoy owned his farms in Beard Township Alfalfa Co., OK (1910); Eden Township, Payne Co., OK (1920); and Autry, Noble County, OK (1930). Children were; Charles Leroy (Roy), Jr. (b. 21 May 1901); Albert Fredrick (Right) (1903-1979); Amy Amelia (1907-1996); Marion Virgil (1908-1913);

Edward (b. 26 April 1909); Clarence (1912-2006); Twins - Allen (1916-2004) and Alvin (1916-1985); Irene Virginia (1918-1958); Joseph Glenn (1920-1936); Claude (1923-1977); and Ernest (1925-1957). Charles LeRoy died in 1964 in OK, USA.

## MARTHA J. "Mattie" FULLER

Born on 1 Feb 1880, Martha J. (Mattie) was a toddler when the family moved to Kansas. The photo shown here was probably taken around 1900 when she was still living in the family home (shown as an "invalid" which may be in error). The 1910 census shows her living with Martha, as a widow, with one daughter, Alta Isaac. Information on her marriage to Mr. Isaac has not been found. She remarried about 1915 to Floyd H. Rogers and they had one son, Winfred, in 1916. Rogers owned a small farm in Morrison, Noble Co., OK, where Mattie died in 1946.

## JOHN VIRGIL FULLER

Born 11 Mar 1882, John Virgil farmed with his mother, Martha, until he married Margaret Abigail at age 29 (about 1911). He then moved to Kiowa, KS and went to work for the Santa Fe Railroad. John Virgil and Margaret Abigail Fuller (right) had at least five children; Ivan R (b. 1913), Ira Leon (b. 1915), Everett W. (b. 1916), Carl V. (b. 1918), and Glenn T. (b. 1921) Abigail died 29 Sep 1966. John Virgil Fuller died in Emporia, KS after her.

## NORA ABIGAIL FULLER

The youngest child of Jonathan Cole and Martha Jane Fuller, Nora Abigail was only six months old when the family moved to Kansas, with no visible sign of support. She married Floyd Adelbert Merryman (a day laborer doing odd jobs) prior to 1910 and is shown living with him in Cherokee Ward 2, Alfalfa Co, OK in the 1910 Census. She died young (Oct 24, 1918 at age 34). Her husband is shown as a farm laborer in Colorado in 1917 when he registered for the W.W. I draft. The 1920 census shows him as a farm laborer (widowed). In 1930 he is a riveter in steel construction, (Colorado), and remarries (Maud A.). They have one child shown living with her mother & grandparents in the 1930 Census.

## Section 4: SARAH ELIZABETH FULLER'S STORY

Sarah Elizabeth Fuller was born on 16 July 1874 in Pendleton, Putnam Co, OH and moved with her parents to Attica in Harper Co, Kansas in the winter of 1885. In Kansas, she met Edward Stanton Watt and they were married by Probate Judge G. H. Alexander in Alva, Woods Co., OK on 31 Dec 1893. It was the same month in which Jonathan and Martha placed their claim in Fritzlen. Edward had staked his claim in September, when the Cherokee Outlet opened. Their marriage certificate lists Sarah as living in Barber County, KS; and Edward as living in Kingfisher Co., Oklahoma (with his sister, Mollie). The marriage license authorized them to marry in Alva, in "M" County in the Oklahoma, later named "Woods" County.

Photo: cc: 1900

Thieves stole their horses, and Edward's claim did not work out; so the young couple was living in Hennessey (perhaps with Edward's sister) in Kingfisher Co., OK when their first child was born, Myrtle Edith, on 18 July 1895. Sarah's next three children were all born in the Winchester-Alva-Hennessey triangle of OK; Edison Jesse (27 July 1897), Effie May (20 Aug 1903), and Bessie Ellen (11 Jan 1906). No records have been found for the family in the 1900 Census, nor documentation of Edward's employment. It may be he worked as a carpenter or laborer. The family moved to Fritzlen, Woods Co, OK where Beulah was born (11 May 1910) and were shown farming there by the 1910 Census. Edward owned his own farm and held a mortgage on the property.

In 1911, Edward, Sarah and children were living in Hardtner, KS once more. Here, Sarah's sixth child, a son named Lee, was born and died on Sept. 12th. He is buried in the Hardtner Cemetery, Lot #39, Block #1. Edward's occupation, listed in the 1915 Kansas census, is "laborer." Following the birth of their two youngest children, Iva Marie (23 Aug 1913) and Naomi Irene (27 Jan 1917) the family moved to Johnson Township, Carter County, in southeastern Missouri in the fall of 1918. The 1920 census shows Edward Watt as a farm laborer working on his own account. By 1930, he owned his own farm in District 7 of Johnson Township and only the two youngest children remained at home. The couple tended to live apart after their children left home. Both remained in the area until their deaths.

Photo: Hardtner, KS, 1912, by John Nixon
Barber County Regional Planning Commission

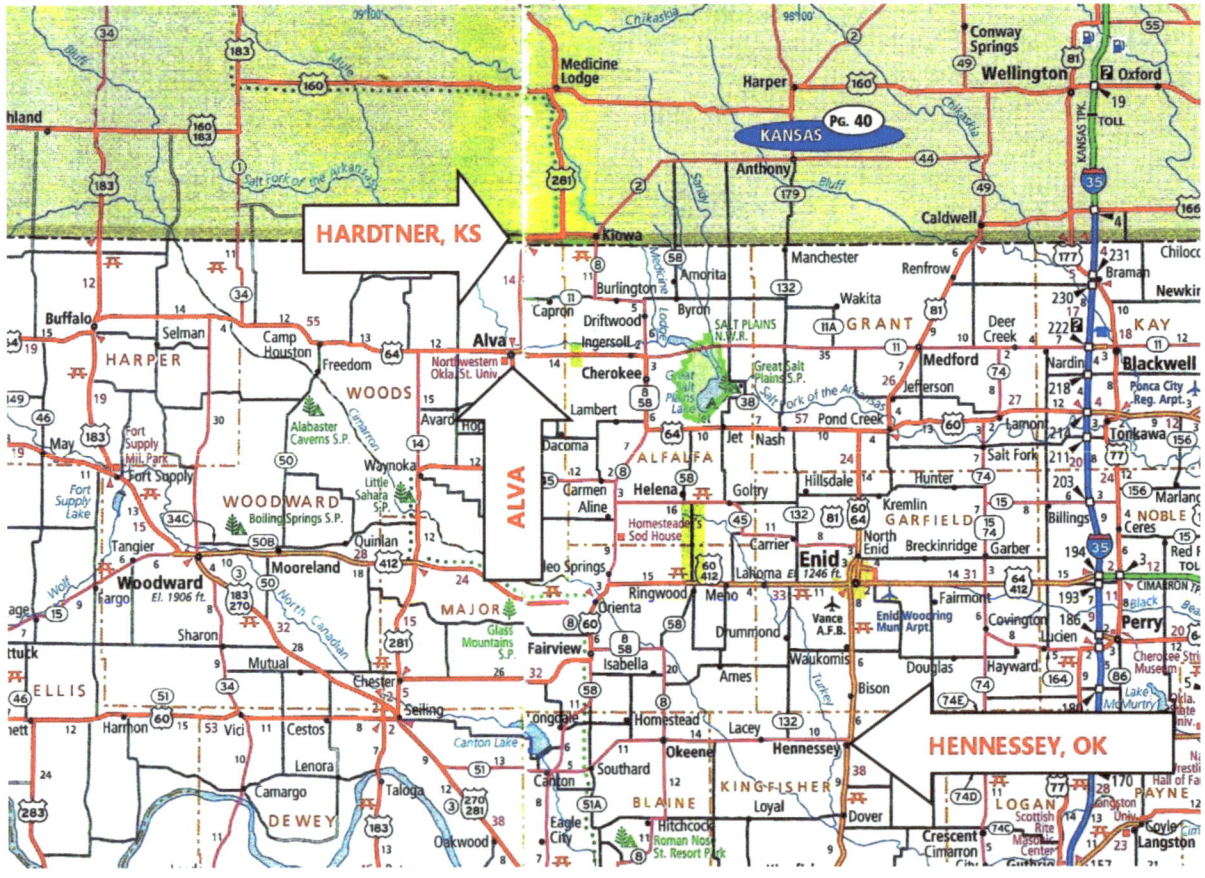

from the Family Bible of Edward & Sara Elizabeth Fuller Watt

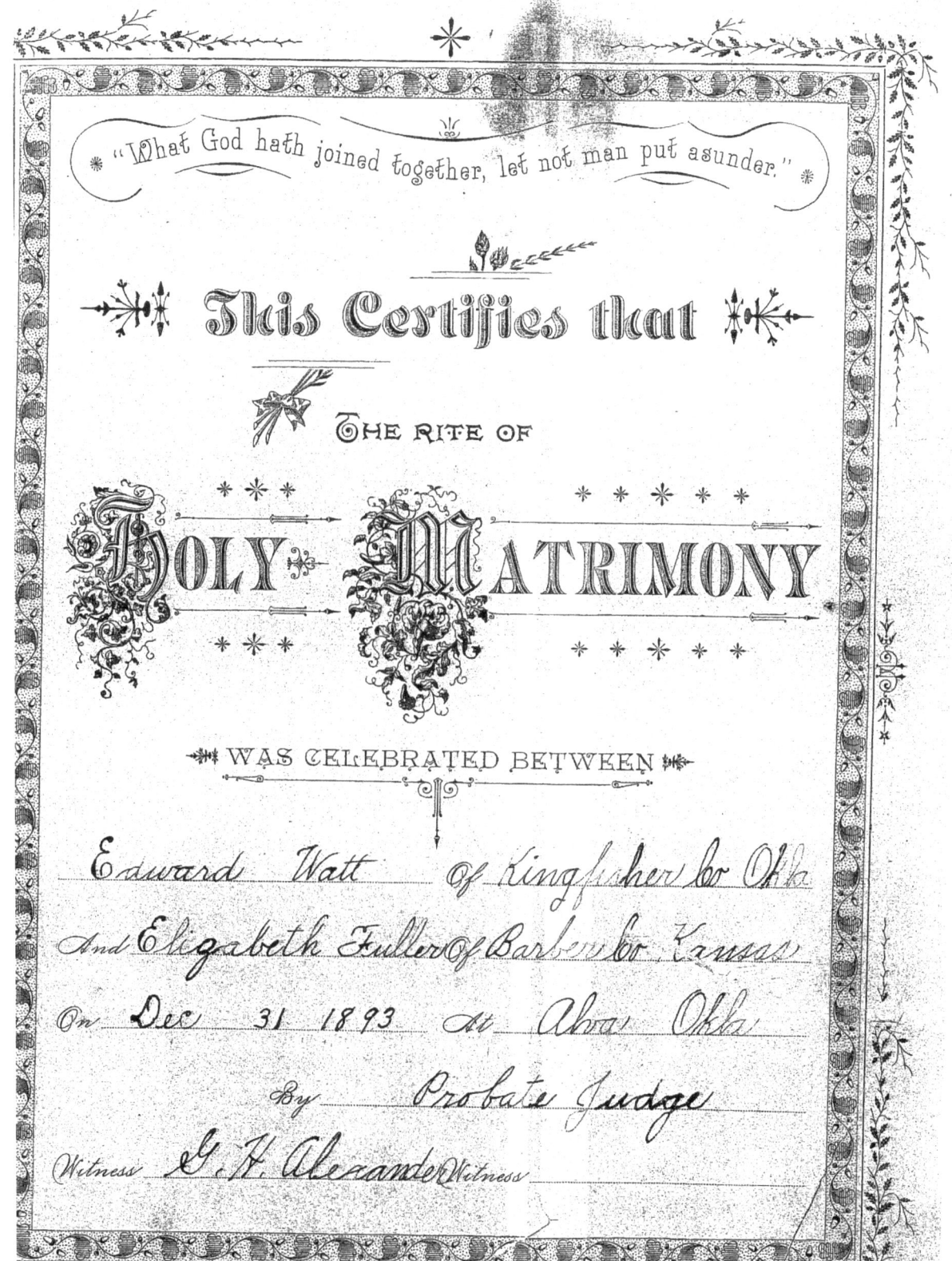

"What God hath joined together, let not man put asunder."

This Certifies that

The Rite of

HOLY MATRIMONY

was celebrated between

Edward Watt of Kingfisher Co Okla
And Elizabeth Fuller of Barber Co Kansas
On Dec 31 1893 At Alva, Okla
By Probate Judge
Witness G. H. Alexander Witness

Sarah lived in Attica, just west of Harper, KS in March 1885. Edward S. Watt's family had moved from Johnson Co, MO to near Wichita, KS in the fall of 1876 and relocated to southwestern Barber County in the fall of 1878. His mother died in 1882 and his father and eldest brother were shot to death by cowboys near Kiowa (east of Hardtner) in June 1884. Edward's sister, Mollie, stayed on her father's claim with the remaining children until losing the land to foreclosure. Then she, too, joined the rush for new land in the Cherokee Outlet. We do not know when the paths of Sarah Elizabeth Fuller and Edward S. Watt first crossed. Nor do we know many of the details of their early life together.

**Sarah and Edward S. Watt (above)**

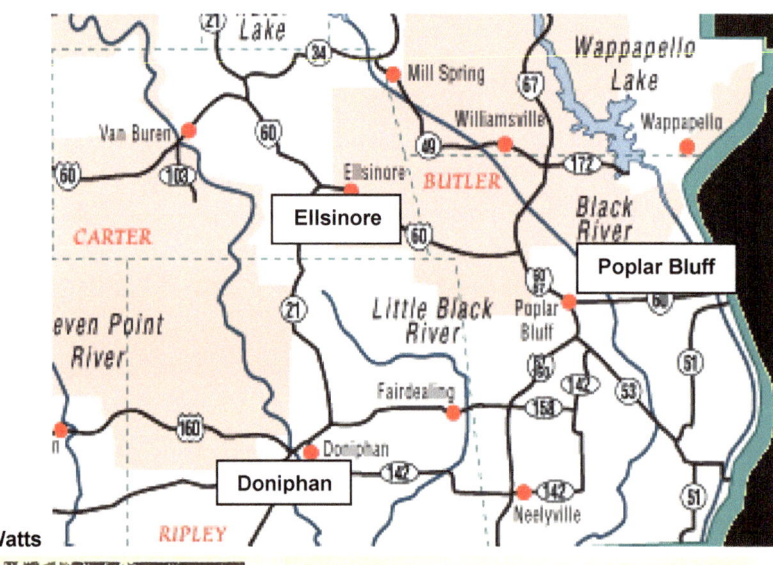

**Later homes of the Watts**

**Photo: 1925, Ellsinore, Carter Co, MO, "The Farm"**

# Standard Certificate of Death

**THE DIVISION OF HEALTH OF MISSOURI**
**FILED APR 6 - 1956**
State File No. 8255
Reg. Dist. No. 43 — Primary Reg. Dist. No. 3007 — Registrar's No. 220

**1. Place of Death**
- a. County: Butler
- b. City or Town: Poplar Bluff
- c. Length of Stay: 3 wks.
- Full Name of Hospital or Institution: Poplar Bluff Hospital

**2. Usual Residence**
- a. State: Missouri
- b. County: Ripley
- c. City or Town: Doniphan
- e. Street Address: Rural Doniphan, Mo.

**3. Name of Deceased:** Sarah Elizabeth Watt
**4. Date of Death:** 3-22-1956
**5. Sex:** Female
**6. Color or Race:** White
**7. Married, Never Married, Widowed, Divorced:** Married
**8. Date of Birth:** 7-16-1874
**9. Age:** 81
**10a. Usual Occupation:** Housewife
**10b. Kind of Business or Industry:** Own Home
**11. Birthplace:** Columbus, Ohio
**12. Citizen of What Country:** USA
**13a. Father's Name:** Jonathan Fuller
**13b. Mother's Maiden Name:** Martha Smith
**14. Name of Husband or Wife:** Edward S. Watt
**15. Was Deceased Ever in U.S. Armed Forces?** No
**16. Social Security No.:** None
**17. Informant's Signature or Name:** Mrs. Baulah Mundis, Poplar Bluff, Mo.

**18. Cause of Death**
- I. Disease or condition directly leading to death: [illegible]
- Antecedent causes: Due to (b) Infect. Gall Bladder
- Due to (c) Stones in gall bladder

**19a. Date of Operation:** —
**20. Autopsy?** No
**22.** I hereby certify that I attended the deceased from 3-14-1956 to 3-22-1956, that I last saw the deceased alive on 3-22-1956, and that death occurred at 9:15 a.m.
**23a. Signature:** [signature], M.D.
**23b. Address:** Poplar Bluff, Mo.
**23c. Date Signed:** 3-26-56
**24a. Burial, Cremation, Removal:** Burial
**24b. Date:** 3-24-56
**24c. Name of Cemetery:** Memorial Gardens
**24d. Location:** Poplar Bluff, Mo.
**Funeral Director:** Greer Croy & Fitch, Poplar Bluff, Mo.
**Date Rec'd by Local Reg.:** 3/16/56

Sarah Elizabeth Fuller (1874-1956)

Sarah's husband, Edward Stanton Watt, is also buried at Memorial Gardens Cemetery near Poplar Bluff, MO. The name of his father on his Death Certificate should read: "Thomas K. Watt." His obituary is reprinted here:

### "EDWARD S. WATT, 'Cherokee Strip' Pioneer, Dies

*Edward Stanton Watt, 93-year-old retired and pioneer Oklahoma homesteader, died at 1:10 a.m. today at his home on Route 2, Poplar Bluff. He had been in failing health for two years and was a resident of the county for 19 years. He was formerly a resident of Ellsinore. Born April 1, 1870, at Warrensburg, MO., he moved to Kansas, setting in the 'Cherokee Strip' and later moved to Wichita, Kan. Before returning to this area. He married Dec. 31, 1898, to the former Miss Sarah Fuller in Oklahoma. She preceded him in death. Among the survivors are the following children: Mrs. Myrtle Johnson, Bolivar; Edison Watt, St. Louis; Mrs. Bessie Condray, McCredie, MO; Mrs. Beulah Mundis, Poplar Bluff; Mrs. Iva Thoman, Wauseon, Ohio, and Mrs. Naomi Whiteside, Waunakee, Wis. There are 16 grandchildren and 24 great grandchildren. Funeral services will be held at 2 p.m. tomorrow in the Greer Croy and Fitch Funeral Chapel. The Rev. Dr. C. E. A. McKim will officiate and burial will be in the Memorial Gardens.*

## SARAH ELIZABETH FULLER-WATT'S CHILDREN

| Name | Occupation | Spouse | Children | Residence(s) | Death & Burial |
|---|---|---|---|---|---|
| Myrtle Edith | Secretary Homemaker | George W. Johnston | 4 | OK, MO, KS, DCA, LA | Jan 2, 1983 Shreveport, LA |
| Edison Jesse | Accountant for Telephone Co. | Floy Alice Smith | 2 | OK,KS,MO | Dec, 1979 Chesterfield, MO |
| Effie May | Bookkeeper Writer | Victor H. Wilder | 0 | OK,KS,MO,MI | May 2, 1936 St. Louis, MO Calhalla Cemetery |
| Bessie Ellen | Homemaker | Lester A. Baetz Lawrence Condray | 2 | OK,KS,MO,MI | Dec, 1993 Kingdom City, MO |
| Beulah Fay | Homemaker | Warren Taft Mundis | 2 | OK, KS, MO, MI | May 23, 2004 Columbia, MO |
| Iva Marie | Homemaker | Charles Joseph Thoman | 3 | KS, MO, MI, OH | Apr 28, 2001 Clark Lake, MI |
| Naomi Irene | Secretary & Farmer | Clyde Clarence Whiteside | 3 | KS, MO, MI, WI, AK, MA | n/a |

## HOMES OF THE WATT CHILDREN AS THEY GREW UP

(Winchester, OK, 1910)

1912-1918, Hardtner, KS

Ellsinore, MO, 1920

Poplar Bluff, MO

The Fuller-Watt children came of age during the Great Depression (1929-1941) in the U.S. Several pursued additional education after graduation from High School. The two oldest children, Edison and Myrtle, raised their families in the St. Louis vicinity. The remaining five daughters all took their office skills to Detroit in the 1930s where they met their future spouses and embarked on their own life journeys.

## MYRTLE EDITH WATT

The eldest of Sarah and Edward's children, Myrtle Edith Watt was born in Hennessey Township, Kingfisher Co., Oklahoma on 18 July 1895. She moved with the family to Hardtner, KS, graduated from high school and then took a job in Woodward, OK. She met her future husband in Woodward, but took a job with the U.S. Treasury in Washington, D.C. during W.W. I, while he served in the military. After their marriage on 19 Oct 1919, the couple lived in Washington, D.C. before returning to St. Louis to raise their family in the 1920s. They had four living children; Mary Lucille (1920-2009), Artemon Paul (1923-2007), George Walter, III (1930-2011), and James Watt (b. 1930). Myrtle died on 2 Jan 1983, in Shreveport, LA.

## EDISON JESSE WATT

Sarah and Edward's only living son, Edison Jesse, was born in northern Oklahoma (probably near Alva) on 27 July 1897. He moved with his family to KS and then to Pike Township in Carter Co., MO, where he was working as a cashier for the Iron Company in the 1920 census. That same year he married Floy Alice Smith (1894-1963). The couple moved to St. Louis where Edison joined the St. Louis Telephone Company as an accountant (1930 census). The couple had two daughters, Elizabeth Jeanette (1922-2004) and Billie L. (1925-2001). Edison died during the month of Dec, 1979, in Chesterfield, St. Louis, Co, MO.

## EFFIE MAY WATT

Born in Alva, OK on 20 Aug 1903, Effie May was the creative writer of the Fuller-Watt family. She graduated from Ellsinore High School and went to St. Louis for additional training, then to Detroit where she worked as an accountant. Effie was active in civic organizations and enjoyed Michigan's outdoor sports. She wrote and published numerous poems about family and life. In particular she gave generous gifts to her younger sisters and encouraged them to begin their careers in Detroit, with her help. In 1935, Effie returned to St. Louis, MO, where she met and married Victor Wilder, an engineer, on Aug 10th of that year. She became ill and died on 2 May 1936 following a kidney operation.

## BESSIE ELLEN WATT

Born in Winchester, OK on 11 Jan 1906, Bessie Ellen (shown on right side of photo) moved to St. Louis, MO in 1923 where she met and married Lester Baetz on 19 Mar 1924. The family moved to Detroit in 1930 where the marriage ended in divorce in 1932. Bessie returned to St. Louis with daughters June (1925-1964) and Lois Anne (1928-2000). She married Lawrence Condray on 2 Jan 1935. Bessie and Lawrence purchased a farmstead near Fulton, MO, where they lived out their lives. Bessie died on 30 Dec 1993 in Callaway County, MO and is buried in Callaway Memorial Gardens in Fulton, MO. (Find A Grave Memorial #76224983)

## BEULAH FAY WATT

Beulah Fay Watt was born in Alva, Oklahoma on 11 May 1910, moving with her family to Hardtner, KS and then to Ellsinore, MO. She received her diploma from Ellsinore High School. In 1928, Beulah went to Detroit, MI to work as a typist for Dossins Food Products. While there she met and married Warren Taft Mundis in Bowling Green, OH on 20 Nov 1930. The couple had a daughter and son (both living). Beulah and her daughter returned to Missouri during WW II, living in Ellsinore and later in Poplar Bluff. After her husband's death in 1970, Beulah entered the School of Practical Nursing and worked at the Doctor's Hospital for several years. In 1989 Beulah moved to Columbia, MO, where she died on 23 May 2004.

## IVA MARIE WATT

The seventh child of Sarah and Edward Watt, Iva Marie Watt was born 23 Aug 1913 in Hardtner, KS. She moved with her family to Ellsinore, MO, then to Overland, MO in 1931. Like her sisters, Iva moved to Detroit, MI for employment and met Charles Joseph Thoman. They were married on 24 May 1941. Three (living) children were born of this marriage. In 1956 the family moved to Brighton, MI, and to Wauseon, OH in 1959. Their final move was to Clarklake, Jackson Co., MI where Iva died at her home on 28 Apr 2001. She is buried in Roseland Memorial Gardens, Jackson, MI.

## NAOMI IRENE WATT

The youngest child of Sarah and Edward Watt, Naomi Irene Watt was born on 27 Jan 1917 in Hardtner, KS. After moving to MO with her family and graduating from Ellsinore High School, Naomi attended a small private college south of St. Louis and then joined her sister Iva in Detroit, MI, taking a secretarial position at Michigan Consolidated Gas Company. She met Clyde C. Whiteside and they were married on 18 Oct 1941. Naomi signed on as a government civil servant in Alaska, where her husband was stationed with the U.S. Army. His Army career took them to many locations; Boston, Chicago, St Louis, Panama Canal Zone, Memphis, and Frankfort, Germany. The couple divorced 18 June 1958 and Naomi and her three (living) children settled on the family farm in Waunakee, WI. Naomi worked as a departmental secretary for the Genetics Dept. at the Univ. of Wis. until her retirement in 1972 at age 55. As of 1 Oct 2011, Naomi still resides on her farm.

## Section 5: THE MISSING LINK, 1785-1805

**"Among a lost list of other Fullers who lived here after the war we find Almon, Abizer, Bartlet, Dayton, Daniel, Jacob, Joseph and Samuel B."** (Whitehall, N.Y., Local History Sketches by Clarence E. Holden)

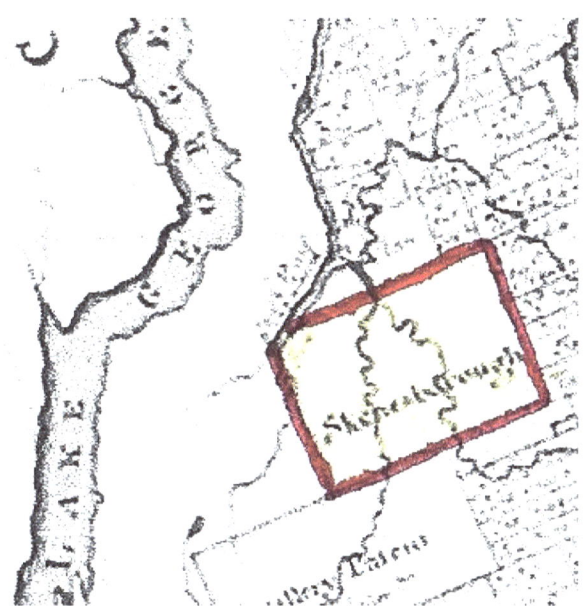

Jacob's sons place him in Whitehall, VT in the early 1800s. The reports are telling for two reasons: 1) They give a specific reference point to study; and 2) they acknowledge the fierce boundary wars that took place before, during and after the Revolutionary War between New York and VT and indicate where the Fuller family's sentiments lay. (There is no Whitehall, VT; it has always been in NY in spite of attempts by Ethan Allen's Green Mountain Boys to have it declared within the border of VT.) The overriding genealogical question has always been – was Jacob Fuller a descendant of Samuel or Edward Fuller, two brothers who arrived in America on board the Mayflower in 1620? For more than 200 years genealogists have been documenting the descendents of these two pilgrims. With the exception of a couple of lines from Edward (that went to Canada and then back to the U.S.), the lineage is fairly complete from MA to NJ, to CT, and up through NY and VT. Unfortunately, none of these *(documented)* lineages include a Jacob Fuller, cc 1785-1872. The CT Fullers did go to Skeneborough, NY (Whitehall) where they were tenant farmers for Philip Skene prior to the Revolutionary War. Skene's lands were confiscated by the Americans and a large contingent of Fuller's remained in the area as landowners and tenant farmers until around 1820, by which time they had moved on to western NY, PA, and OH. It is possible Jacob Fuller (1785-1872) was related in some way to these Fullers, many of whom settled initially in northern OH, however no documents exist to record the fact. There were also Evans in the Whitehall area (possible ancestors of Lucy Evans), but that documentation is also lacking.

Whitehall, Fort Edward, and Fort Ann were the scene of many military conflicts during both the Revolutionary War and the War of 1812. Records were either not kept, or destroyed by numerous fires in public offices. In spite of the fact that, *"By intermarriages the Fullers were related to most of the early families of the town....All of the Fullers, except John and Ephriam, drop out of the records after 1817, and those two follow a couple of years later."* (Whitehall, N.Y., Local History Sketches by Clarence E. Holden)

Two tidbits of information remain: 1) New York Genealogical Records that show a Jacob Fuller living in Hebron, Washington Co., NY (near Whitehall) in 1800; 2) the long-lost list containing the name of a Jacob Fuller who left Whitehall circa 1812 and settled in Ohio. It is possible additional information and research may one day be able to expand on these two points.

The process of elimination leaves at least one possible, (*documented*) plausible, chronological route to Jacob's ancestors. This route centers on a Jacob Fuller born in Sacksville, Nova Scotia, Canada, 1766-1830(6); son of Jacob Fuller, 1734-1800(5); son of Samuel Fuller, 1702-1788(4); son of Samuel Fuller, 1675-1724(3); son of Samuel Fuller, 1649-1676(2); son of immigrant Robert Fuller 1616-1706(1). A brief description of Robert Fuller (1616-1706) follows.

Robert FULLER Of Salem and Rehoboth was born about 1616 in Southampton, Hampshire, England. He died on 10 May 1706 in Rehoboth, Bristol, Massachusetts. Robert Fuller was born about 1615 perhaps in Suffolk or Norfolk county near the southeastern coast of England. Most everyone with the surname of "Fuller" lived in this region when the name first came into use because it was where the woolen cloth manufacturers were located. The name comes from the trade of "fuller." A fuller's job was important to the refinement of finished cloth. A fuller scoured wool and other cloth after it was woven to make it whiter, tighter, thicker, and more durable. In part of his process, the fuller would sprinkle the woven cloth with a clay called "fuller's earth", then fold and soak the cloth in a tub of water. While in the tub, he would walk on the cloth with his bare feet to even out the fill. In 1638, Robert Fuller is said to have sailed from the port of Southampton to Salem, which was in the English-chartered, Massachusetts Bay Colony. His passage was probably on the ship "Bevis of Hampton." The Bevis made only one voyage to America and Robert's name does not appear in the ship's manifest. However, he may have worked for his passage as an ordinary seaman, in which case, his name would not have appeared among those of the regular passengers. At the time of his arrival, colonial Salem was twelve years old. There were already several other Fullers living in Massachusetts when Robert arrived. Some had sailed with the Puritans from England to Plymouth Rock in 1620 on the Mayflower. It has not been shown using civil records that Robert was in fact related to these other Fullers, but it is remotely possible. If Robert was related to brothers Samuel and Edward Fuller, or Susanna (Fuller) White of the Mayflower, then he was probably a nephew. If so, he would have been the son of Thomas Fuller, who remained in England. Robert may also have had an older brother named Thomas who came to Massachusetts in 1638, but lived first in Woburn and then in Salem. Again, no proof has been found yet of this relationship. Robert married Sarah Bowen at Salem in about 1639. She was born in Wales in about 1616 to Richard and Ann Bowen. The entire Bowen family was living in Salem--already a busy seaport--by the time Robert arrived. In 1645, however, Robert was given land in Rehoboth, which was in an unsettled area to the southwest of Salem about 60 miles away. By 1650, he had moved his family there. Robert and Sarah had six children: Jonathan, Elizabeth, John, Samuel, Abigail, and Benjamin. He and Sarah built a new home at the southwest end of a scenic area called the "Ring of Green" which was on the Seekonk plain. The family lived there for about the next twenty

-five years, until serious problems with Indian attacks made life there intolerable. Today this land is part of East Providence, Rhode Island. During his first years in America, Robert made his living as a bricklayer. He is mentioned many times in this regard in the early records of Town meetings of both Salem and Rehoboth. In those days, a bricklayer's job consisted mainly of building fireplaces, bake ovens, chimneys, foundations, and cellar walls. Houses were not generally brick, but were back-plastered with lime on the walls and ceilings for greater warmth. At first, a bricklayer in Massachusetts had his pay set by the Court of Assistants; In 1630, the order had been that carpenters, joiners, sawyers, bricklayers, and thatchers could be paid no more than two shillings a day. This order was repealed, however, because it failed to promote the skilled labor which was vital to the growing colony. Robert did not become a "freeman" until 1655. Unless you were granted the status of freeman, you could not vote or hold public office. In order to be a freeman in the Plymouth Colony, however, you had to be approved by the minister of the congregation--in Massachusetts this meant you had to be a Puritan. Indeed, Robert was a loyal Congregationalist, and received his grant. Later, in 1668, he and his brother-in-law were elected constables for one year. "Att the General Court of Elections held att Plymouth the third Day of June, Anno Dom 1668, Prence Gour, Constables of Rehoboth-- Robert ffuller George Kendricke" Constables kept the peace, made arrests, served warrants, and among other popular activities, collected taxes. In 1675 and 1676, Rehoboth was attacked several times by the Wampanoag Indians in what was called "King Philip's War." Scores of townspeople were ambushed in the fields or killed in surprise attacks by angry natives. King Philip, or "Metacomet" (which was his Indian name), was the son of Massasoit, chief of the Wampanog tribe. Apparently, the Indians had become increasingly angry with the encroachments of the early settlers, and resorted to violence. As a result of these attacks, Robert lost his wife, Sarah, and three of his children, John, Samuel, and Abigail. His daughter Elizabeth lost her husband, Nehemiah Sabin. Shortly after these tragic losses, Robert returned to Salem. Soon he remarried to Margaret Waller, whose husband had also been killed. Margaret and Robert lived in Salem until the late 1690s. Fortunately for them, they were not among the 125 persons accused of witchcraft in 1692. After trial, many witches were hanged. (None was ever burned.) The governor of the Massachusetts colony finally put a stop to the incredible nonsense in 1693. Eventually, Robert went back to Rehoboth to live out his last years with his grown children. Margaret died about 1700 and Robert in 1706. They are both probably buried in the oldest cemetery in Rehoboth.

[Much of the above was based on information provided by Clarence C. Fuller in his book "Robert Fuller of Salem"] He was married to Sarah BOWEN in 1639 in Salem, Massachusetts Bay Colony.

http://freepages.genealogy.rootsweb.ancestry.com/~smason/combined/nti05208.htm

Complicating the lack of records to either confirm or refute the linkage between Jacob Fuller, 1785-1872(7) and Jacob Fuller, 1766-1830(6) is the fact that his father, Jacob Fuller, 1734-1800(5) named two of his sons "Jacob". The first son Jacob Fuller, 1766-1830(6) was born in Sackville, Nova Scotia, Canada while his parents participated in the "New England Planters" movement to resettle land in Canada left vacant when the British drove the French out of the Nova Scotia area in the mid-1700s. He had five sisters and one brother. By 1770, the family returned to Rehoboth, MA and Jacob (5) fought in the Revolutionary War. In 1791, Jacob's mother (Deborah Tower) died. His father, Captain Fuller, 1734-1800(5), remarried the widow Sarah Goodall on 22 Aug 1791. Their only child, a son born on 30 Mar 1792, was also named Jacob. Jacob (6.2) and his mother applied for the pension of Jacob(5) after his death, but their application was denied. Jacob, 1766-1830(6), settled in New Haven, Addison Co., VT where he and his (second?) wife Patty are buried in Riverside Cemetery. The names of his children remain to be discovered. Perhaps future DNA studies will provide the final answers.

**CLARIFICATIONS:**

No documentation was found to connect Jacob Fuller (1785-1872) with the Fullers of Jefferson and Lewis Counties, NY, who fought during the War of 1812.

Jacob Winegar Fuller, b. 1786 in NY, is not our Jacob Fuller. Jacob W. Fuller was born 17 Nov 1786 in Dutchess County, NY, USA and died 5 Jan 1867 in DuPage Co, Illinois. This Jacob Fuller did not settle in Ohio...he and wife Candance went from NY to Illinois in the spring of 1835 and became a land developer for what would become Oak Brook, IL. He is buried in Fullersberg Cemetery, DuPage Co, IL, Lot 29.

There were many Jacob Fullers in New York following the Revolution. Attempts to track their movement and residence, however, showed none that moved to Ohio, other than the one whose lineage we seek.

# APPENDIX A – FULLERS IN UNIFORM

**CIVIL WAR**

| Serviceman | Lineage | Unit | Date(s) Served | Description |
|---|---|---|---|---|
| Albert (1844-1817) | Samuel, Jacob | Co C, 68th OVI | 1861-1865 | Enlisted (Pvt) at age 18, Oct 31, 1861 to serve 3 yrs. Mustered out on 10 July 1865. Buried Section 17, Lot 66, Grave 7, Sherman Cemetery, Brown Twnshp, Paulding Co, OH |
| Harry, Rev. (1840-1923) | Jacob | Co I, 88th OVI | 1863-1865 | Enlisted (Pvt) at age 23, 4 July 1863 to serve 3 yrs. Appt Corporal. Mustered out on 3 July 1865. Buried Prairie Chapel Cemetery, Section 25-26, Row 4, Grave 57. |
| Jacob (1846-1928) | Abel, Jacob | Co I, 88th OVI | 1863-1865 | Enlisted (Pvt) at age 17, 30 July 1863. Mustered out 4 July 1865. Disability incurred, chronic diarrhea. |
| Jacob E. (1838-N/A) | Jacob | Co L, 3rd Reg. OH Calvary | 1863-1865 | Enlisted (Pvt) at age 25, 1 July 1863. Mustered out 4 Aug 1865. |
| Jacob Willis (1839-1918) | Matthew, Jacob | Co D, 189th Reg, OVI | 1865 | Enlisted (Pvt) at age 26, 11 Feb 1865, Co D, 189th Reg. OVI. Mustered out 28 Sep 1865. |
| Jonathan Cole (1837-1905) | Abel, Jacob | Co F, 25th OVI & Co C, 151st OVI | 1861-1864 | Enlisted (Pvt) at age 24, 20 June 1861, Co F, 25th OVI; POW on 15 Jan 1862, released & received Surgeon's Certif. of Disability 13 Oct 1862 (chronic diarrhea). Re-enlisted 2 May 1864, Co C, 151st OVI. Discharged 27 Aug 1864. Buried Fairview Cemetery, Woods Co., OK, Row 3, Lot 4. |
| Reuben Martin (1841-1862) | Matthew, Jacob | Co K, 14th OVI | 1861-1862 | Enlisted (Pvt) at age 20, 25 Aug 1861; injured in battle & died in hospital in Corinth, MS, 5 July 1862. |
| William Robert (1843-1925) | Matthew, Jacob | Co K, 14th OVI | 1861-1865 | Enlisted (Pvt) at age 18, 25 Aug 1861, Co K, 14th OVI. Promoted to Corporal, 1 Oct 1864. Mustered out 11 July 1865. Disability, Scurvey. Buried, Truro Cemetery (north side) Putnam Co, OH, Row 5, Grave 13. |
| Willis A. (1939-1928) | Samuel, Jacob | Co G, 14th OVI & Co C, 68th OVI | 1861-1865 | Enlisted (Pvt) at age 22, 22 Oct 1861, to serve 3 yrs. Mustered out 27 June 1865. Buried in Sherman Cemetery, Brown Twnshp, Paulding Co, OH, Section 17, Lot 27, Grave 7. |

Guns of Fort Donelson on the Cumberland River, TN (Photo by K. L. Houk, October 2011)

## MILITARY UNITS OF THE CIVIL WAR SERVED BY DESCENDENTS OF JACOB FULLER

### CALVARY:  3rd Ohio Volunteer Cavalry

This Regiment was organized from the State at large, at Monroeville, Huron County, Ohio, from September 4, 1861 to December 11, 1861, to serve three years.

On the expiration of their term of service, the original members (except veterans) were mustered out, and the organization composed of veterans and recruits was retained in service until August 4, 1865, when it was mustered out in accordance with orders from the War Department.

### INFANTRY:  14th Ohio Volunteer Infantry

This Regiment was organized at Toledo, Ohio from August 14-September 5, 1861, to serve three years. On the expiration of term of service the original members (except veterans) were mustered out and the organization, composed of veterans and recruits, retained in the service until July 11, 1865, when it was mustered out in accordance with orders from the War Department.

### 25th Ohio Volunteer Infantry

This Regiment was organized at Columbus, Ohio in June and July 1861 to serve three years. Company D was permanently detached as the 12th Battery, Ohio Light Artillery, March 17, 1862. A new company was organized in October 1864 to serve one year and assigned to this Regiment as Company D. The original members (except veterans) were mustered out on July 16, 1864 and Company D October 16, 1865, by reason on expiration of term of service. The organization, composed of veterans and recruits, was retained in service until June 18, 1866 when it was mustered out in accordance with orders from the War Department.

### 68th Ohio Volunteer Infantry

This Regiment was organized in the State of Ohio at large, from October through December 1861 to serve three years. On the expiration of its term of service, the original members (except veterans) were mustered out, and the organization, composed of veterans and recruits, retained in service until July 10, 1865, when it was mustered out in accordance with orders from the War Department.

## 88th Ohio Volunteer Infantry

This Regiment was originally composed of a battalion of four companies, organized at Camp Chase, Ohio, from September 24 to October 27, 1862, to serve three years, as designated "1st Battalion Governor's Guards."

Six new companies were organized at Camp Chase, Ohio, from July 24 to August 3, 1863, to serve three years, and consolidated with this battalion and designated 88th Ohio Volunteers. It was mustered out of service July 3, 1865, in accordance with orders from the War Department.

This Regiment was principally engaged in guarding Rebel prisoners at Camp Chase, Ohio. It was also engaged in the pursuit of the Morgan raiders and the suppression of the Holmes County rebellion, in July 1863.

## 151st Ohio Volunteer Infantry

This Regiment was organized at Camp Chase, Ohio, May 13, 1864, to serve 100 days. It was composed of the 53rd Regiment, Ohio National Guard, from Allen County, and the 57th Battalion, Ohio National Guard from Hocking County. On the 14th of May the Regiment left Camp Chase for Washington, DC, via Ohio Central and Baltimore Railroads. It reached Washington on the 21st of May and reported to General Augur. The reiment was first stationed at Forst Sumner, Mansfield, and Simmons. During the active operations of the Rebels against Washington, on the 11th and 12th of July, the larger part of the Regiment was under fire. Several of the companies were in forts which were engaged in the battle. companies C and G were at Fort Stevens, Company I at Battery Smeade, and Company K at Fort Kearney. On the 17th of August orders were received to concentrate the Regiment at Fort Simmons. From this place the Regiment moved, via Baltimore and Pittsburgh, to Camp Chase, where it arrived on the 23rd. It was mustered out August 27, 1864, on expiration of its term of service.

## 188th Ohio Volunteer Infantry

This Regiment was organized at Camp Chase, Ohio, March 2-4, 1865 to serve one year. On March 4, the Regiment received orders to report to General Thomas at Nashville, TN, where it arrived on the 9th. It was assigned to duty under Brigadier Genera Van Cleve, and ordered to Murfreesboro, TN, where it remained two months, and was then ordered to Nashville, TN, where it remained until September 21, 1865, when it was\ mustered out in accordance with orders from the War Department.

## 189th Ohio Volunteer Infantry

This Regiment was organized at Toledo, Camp Chase, Cincinnati, Marietta, Hillsboro, and Dayton, Ohio from January 12 to March 6, 1865 to serve one year. On the 4th of March the Regiment was ordered to report to General Thomas at Nashville, where it arrived on the 9th. It was assigned to duty, under Brigadier General Van Cleve, and ordered to Murfreesboro, TN, where it remained two months, and was then ordered to Tullahoma. Here it remained two months, and was then ordered to Nashville, where it remained until September 28, 1865, when it was mustered out in accordance with orders from the War Department.

## OTHER (KNOWN) MILITARY SERVICE

| Serviceman | Lineage | Unit | Dates | Description |
|---|---|---|---|---|
| Herman D Fuller | | WWI, Army Co D, 47th BN, CG | 1918-1919 | 158 Depot Brigade to 24 Sep 1918; Co D 45 Battalion, U.S. Guards to Discharge Sergeant, 1 Oct 1918, Honorable discharge, 28 Feb, 1919 |
| Harry S Fuller | | US Navy | 1926-1930 | |
| Clyde Fuller | Marvin C, | US Air Force | | Aviation Mechanic, killed in Burma, 25 Jan 1944 |
| Riley Ellis | James Edward, Rev. Harry, Jacob | 156st Hospital | 1941 | |
| Wilbur E Fuller | | WW II | 1945 | |
| Glenn E Fuller | | WW II, Sgt US Army | | Buried in Economy Cemetery, El Dorado, KS 67042 (Death, 13 Oct 2003) |
| Mary L Johnston | | | | |
| Artemon P Johnston | | | | |
| | | | | |

# APPENDIX B – DECENDENTS OF JACOB FULLER (1785-1872)

1. Jacob Fuller b: abt 1785 d: abt 1872
    + Lucy Evans b: abt 1786 d: abt 1830
    2. Abel B. Fuller b: 2 July 1805 d: 5 June 1856
        + Roxana Cole b: abt 1809 d: Apr 1840
            3. Orson D Fuller b: 30 Jul 1829 d: 28 Sep 1899
                + Ellen Mayberry b: 1833 d: 1853
                    4. Nancy M. Fuller b: 1 Jan 1921
                        + Jonas Closson
                        + Jacob Marquart
                + Mary Jamison b: 14 July 1829 d: 24 Nov 1859
                    4. John Francis Fuller b: 27 Aug 1854 d: 1932
                    4. Alexander Theodore Fuller b: 13 Dec 1857 d: 1940
                + Cynthia Bussart b: 1833 d: 1900
                    4. Mary A Fuller b: 4 Mar 1862 d: 19 Dec 1944
                    4. Julia E Fuller b: 7 Apr 1864
                    4. Rachel Fuller b: 25 Aug 1865 d: 29 Nov 1878
            3. infant daughter b: 19 Apr 1833
            3. Sarah Ann Fuller b: 10 Oct 1834 d: 12 July 1852
                + William P Bowers b: 1819
                    4. Elizabeth Ellen Bowers b: 1848 d: 1864
                    4. Abel Fuller Bowers b: 1850
            3. Harless C Fuller     b: 23 June 1834 d: before 1880
                + Mary E Farmer b: 1833
                    4. Charles Fuller b: 1861
                    4. Samuel Fuller b: 1864
                    4. Alvada Fuller b: 1866
                    4. Alvira A Fuller b: 1867
                        + Samuel Busich
                    4. Marion Fuller b: 1869
            3. Jonathan Cole Fuller b: 29 Sep 1837  d: 16 Nov 1905
                + Martha Jane Smith b: 23 July 1845  d: 26 Dec 1928
                    4. Mary Anna Fuller b: 5 Apr 1876 d: 10 Jan 1877
                    4. Alice Roxana Fuller b: 12 July 1864 d: 20 June 1891
                        + Mr. Boggess
                    4. Katherine Sevilla Fuller b: 24 Nov 1865 d: 5 Jan 1867
                    4. William Benjamen Fuller  b: 18 Dec 1867 d: 2 Sep 1906
                        + Esther Annie Brooks
                    4. Thomas Benton Fuller b: 19 Sep 1869 d: 9 Nov 1878
                    4. Elizabeth Alberta Fuller b: 17 Sep 1871 d: 13 July 1956
                        + Joseph Sneary b: 1867 d: 1946
                            5. Gladys Sneary b: 1897 d: 1957
                                + Clay Potter
                            5. Grace Sneary b: 1898
                                + Mr. Phillips ?

4. Joseph Clenton Fuller b: 23 Apr 1873 d: 1958
   + Edithy Myrtle Cline  b: 1875 d: 1962
      5. Olean Theadore Fuller b: 22 Feb 1898 d: Sep 1985
      5. Alma Royal Fuller b: 9 Nov 1900 d:29 Sep 1995
         + Ernest Franklin Sheddy b: 1901 d: 1961
            6. Joan Kay Sheddy b: 1938 d: 1979
      5. Robert Fuller b: & d: 23 April 1903
      5. Verne D Fuller b: 23 Dec 1904
      5. Harold Earl Fuller b: 30 May 1907 d: 10 Oct 1991
      5. Helen Fuller b: 9 June 1909 d: 16 Oct 1992
4. Sarah Elizabeth Fuller b: 16 July 1874 d: 22 Mar 1956
   + Edward Stanton Watt b: 1 Apr 1870 d: 11 Nov 1963
      5. Myrtle E Watt b: 18 July 1895 d: 2 Jan 1983
         + George W Johnston b: 1896 d: 1989
            6. Artemon Johnston b: 1923 d: 2007
               + Corienne Kuehnle b: 1925 d: 1989
            6. Mary Lucille Johnston b: 1920 d: 2009
               + Loren Nussbaum b: 1926 d: 1995
            6. Living
            6. George Johnston b: 1930 d: 2011
               + Pat
      5. Edison Jesse Watt b: 27 July 1897 d: Dec 1979
         + Floy Alice Smith b: 1893 d:1963
            6. Elizabeth Jeanette Watt b: 1922 d: 2004
               + Errell T Orear b: 1918 d: 1986
            6. Billie Lou Watt b: 1925 d: 2001
               + Harold Arthur Studer b: 1923
      5. Effie May Watt b: 20 Aug 1903 d: 2 May 1936
         + Victor H Wilder
      5. Bessie Ellen Watt b: 11 Jan 1906 d: Dec 1993
         +Lester A Baetz b: 1901
            6. June Baetz b: 1925 d: 1964
            6. Lois Baetz b: 1928 d: 2000
         + Lawrence Condray
      5. Beulah Fay Watt b: 11 Mar 1910 d: 23 May 2004
         + Warren Taft Mundis  b:1908 d: 1970
            6. Living
            6. Living
      5. Infant Lee Watt b: 12 Sep 1912 d: 1912
      5. Iva Marie Watt b: 23 Aug 1912 d: 28 Apr 2001
         + Charles Joseph Thoman  b:1914 d: 2009
            6. Living
            6. Living
            6. Living
      5. Naomi Irene Watt b: 27 Jan 1917
         + Clyde Clarence Whiteside 14 Jan 1912 d: 23 Mar 2007
            6. Living
            6. Living
            6. Living

    4. Mary Anna Fuller  b: 5 Apr 1876  d: 10 Jan 1877
    4. Charles LeRoy Fuller  b: 29 Nov 1877  d: 1964
     + Sarah Rebecca Lowden  b: 19 Aug 1881  d: 3 Nov 1968
      5. Amy Amelia Fuller  b: 8 Mar 1907  d: 30 Dec 1996
       + George Ivy Dennis  b: 18 July 1872  d: 1942
      5. Charles Leroy Fuller, Jr.  b: 21 May 1901
      5. Albert Fredrick Fuller  b:7 Mar 1903  d: Dec 1979
      5. Marion Virgil Fuller  b: 22 Mar 1908  d: 18 Oct 1913
      5. Edward Fuller  b: 26 Apr 1909
      5. Clarence Fuller  b: 21 June 1912  d: 15 May 2006
      5. Allen Fuller  b: 28 Feb 1916  d: 2004
      5. Alvin Fuller  b: 28 Feb 1916  d: 1985
      5. Irene Virginia Fuller  b: 23 June 1918  d: Mar 1958
      5. Joseph Glenn Fuller  b: 24 Dec 1920  d: 10 July 1986
      5. Claude Fuller  b: 26 June 1923  d: 1977
      5. Ernest Fuller  b: 30 May 1925  d: 1957
    4. Martha Jane Fuller  b: 1 Feb 1880  d: 1946
     + Mr. Isaac
      5. Alta Isaac  b: 1902
     + Floyd H Rogers
      5 Winfred  b: 1916
    4. John Virgil Fuller  b: 11 Mar 1882
    4. Nora Abigail Fuller  b: 9 Sep 1884  d: 24 Oct 1918
     + Mr. Merryman
+ Prudence Rachel Mayberry  b: 29 Nov 1807  d: 30 Oct 1846
  3. William Fuller  b: 15 June 1841  d: 1 Aug 1841
  3. Louisa Fuller  b: 28 Apr 1842  d: 30 Nov 1909
   + William Timbers
    4. Theodore A Timbers  b: 1864  d: 1929
    4. Rosetta Timbers  b: 1868
    4. Jesse  A Timbers  b: 1876
    4. Eddie Timbers  b: 1884
  3. Nancy Elizabeth Fuller  b: 26 May 1843
   + Miles Barfell  b: 29 Mar 1838  d: 25 Nov 1871
    4. Louisa Barfell  b: 1861
    4. Mary Ellen Barfell  b: 1862
    4. Thomas Barfell  b: 1864
    4. William Barfell  b: 1868
    4. Miles LeRoy Barfell  b: 1873  d: 1934
  3. Lucy Fuller  b: 4 Aug 1845  d: 9 Dec 1917
   + Thomas I Louthan
    4. John M Louthan  b: 1863
    4. Marietta J Louthan  b: 1865
    4. Jesse B Louthan  b: 1867
    4. George Bird Louthan  b: 1871  d: 1960
    4. Mary E Louthan  b: 1874  d: 1876
    4. Lizzie C Louthan  b: 1878
    4. Orson R Louthan  b: 1880

                4. Adolpha Brooks  b: 1883  d: 1980
        3. Jacob Fuller  b: 4 Oct 1846  d: 1928
            + Isabell Hubble  b: 1848  d: 1921
                4. Thomas Fuller  b: 1871
                4. Grace Fuller  b: 1879
                4. Edward Eugene Fuller  b: 1882
                4. Homer J Fuller  b: 1889
                4. Oma F Fuller  b: 1900
        3. Jesse E Fuller  b: 20 July 1847  d: Bef 1850
    + Catherine Ann Pence  b: 1827  d: 12 Aug 1870
        3. Infant son Fuller  b: 29 Oct 1848  d: 19 Nov 1848
        3. Mary Ellen Fuller  b: 6 June 1850  d: 8 Nov 1933
            + Johnson M Smith  b: 1846  d: 1913
                4. Olive Smith  b: 1870
                4. John Smith  b: 1872
                4. Elizabeth L Smith  b: 1874
                4. Myrtle Anna Smith  b: 1876  d: 1963
                4. Harry A Smith  b: 1878
                4. Frank R Smith  b: 1880
                4. Emma Bertha Smith  b: 1882  d: 1973
                4. Blaine Smith  b: 1884
                4. Lorenzo Smith  b: 1887  d: 1889
        3. Phoebe Roxana Fuller  b: 24 Apr 1853  d: 15 Mar 1923
            + James Bracy  b: 1852  d: 1940
                4. George E Bracy  b: 1877
                4. Harry Bracy  b: 1878
                4. John Bracy  b: 1882
                4. Aurora A Bracy  b: 1886
                4. Aaroca Bracy  b: 1887
                4. Rosa Bracy  b: 1887
                4. Orpha Bracy  b: 1890  d: 1951
        3. Abel B Fuller, Jr.  b: 11 Jan 1856  d: 11 May 1856
2. Matthew Fuller  b: 1809  d: 1859
    + Elizabeth Abigail Durfee  b: 1816  d: 1893
        3. Jacob W Fuller  b: 1839  d: 26 Apr 1918
            + Melissa Jane Norton  b: 1842  d: 23 Dec 1909
                4. Elizabeth Fuller  b: 1868
                  +Mr. Treece
                4. Viola Fuller  b: 1870
                4. John R Fuller  b: 22 Aug 1872  d: 22 Jan 1946
                    + Emma Dangler
                4. Edward Freeman Fuller  b: 1880  d: 1955
                4. Ruth L Fuller  b: 1883
                4. Homer Fuller
        3. Reuben M Fuller  b: 1841  d: 1862
        3. William R Fuller  b: June 1843  d: 9 July 1925
            + Mary Elizabeth Gobin  b: 1850  d: 1904
                4. Edward Fuller  b: 1870
                4. Harrie C Fuller  b: 1877

    4. Harry Thayer Fuller b: 1878
2. Anna Fuller b: 1811 d: abt 1860
 + Elisha Crandall b: 1799
   3. Wiliam H Crandall b: 1827
   3. Lois Ann Crandall b: 1832 d: 1913
   3. Samuel Crandall b: 1839
   3. Caroline Crandall b: 1841 d: 1916
   3. Marena Crandall b: 1844
   3. Maranda Crandall b: 1846
   3 Zachara T Crandall b: 1848
2. Samuel Fuller b: 12 Nov 1812 d: 18 Mar 1890
 + Eunice Miriah Ashley b: 17 Mar 1817 d: 11 Apr 1901
   3. Willis A Fuller b: 31 Mar 1839 d: 1 July 1928
    + Nancy Agnus Burt b: 1848 d: 1923
     4. Marvin Casper Fuller b: Dec 1866 d: 12 Dec 1964
      + Edith M Harger b: 1867 d: 1932
       5 Ethel M Fuller b: 1886 d: 1967
       5. Essie A Fuller b: 1888
       5. Glenna E Fuller b: 1893
       5. Marshall Dewey Fuller b: 15 Oct 1897 d: 11 Mar 1942
       5. Adin Chloyde Fuller b: 1900 d: 1982
        + Florence Velma Ross b: 9 Aug 1902 d: 8 Mar 1932
         6. Robert Fuller
         6. Raymond Fuller
         6. Donald Fuller
       5. Clyde R Fuller b: 1902 d: 25 Jan 1944
       5. Floyd G Fuller b: 1905
       5. Lola Merle Fuller b: 1908 d: 1918
       5. Lynn Fuller b: 1909
       5. Lawrence Albert Fuller b: 1915 d: 1935
     4. Ernest A Fuller b: 1870 d: 14 Dec 1937
      + Viola Fuller b: 1874
       5. Melva M Fuller b: 1897
       5. Gabbert A Fuller b: 1908
       5. Talbert Fuller b: 1909
       5. Ernstine Fuller b: 1911
       5. Willis Fuller b: 1915
     4. Minnie A Fuller b: 1874 d: 1958
   3. Martha A Fuller b: 15 Oct 1840 d: 20 Apr 1841
   3. Isaac A Fuller b: 9 July 1842 d: 10 July 1844
   3. Albert Fuller b: 10 Sep 1844 d: 24 June 1917
    + Dora Rouse Rathburn b: 28 June 1856 d: 1946
     4. George Bird Fuller
      + Della Shisler b: 1888 d:1964
       5. Mildred Fuller
       5. Warren Fuller
       5. Lloyd Fuller
   3. Happalonia Fuller b: 3 Aug 1847 d: 18 Mar 1939
   3. Ellen Ada Fuller b: 27 Sep 1851 d: 17 Oct 1851

    3. Elllen Adell Fuller   b: 27 Sep 1851   d: 29 Oct 1851
  2. Quartus (Cortez) Fuller   b: 1817   d: bef 1860
   + Elizabeth Norton   b: 1818
    3. Sylvia Fuller   b: 1843
    3. Rosanna Fuller   b: 1844   d: 1916
    3. Clarissa/Melissa Fuller   b: 1846
    3. Garrison Fuller   b: 1849
  2: Calvin Fuller   b: 1819   d: 1878
   + Susan Campbell   b: 1824
    3. Emily Fuller   b: 1841
    3. Almeda Fuller   b: 1843
    3. William Fuller   b: 1856   d: 1856
  2. Daughter Fuller   b: bef 1820
  2. Orphelia (Orpha) Fuller   b: 1823   d: abt 1865
   + Joe Belden (Jabez Devatus)   b: 1817   d: 1870
    3. Isahel Albert Goodrich Belden   b: 1843   d: 1886
    3. Cornelia Beldon   b: 1844
    3. Alfred M Beldon   b: 1847
    3. Henry Andrew Belden   b: 1848
    3. Willis Belden   b: 1851
    3. Phoebe Roxanne Belden   b: 1853   d: 1920
    3. Charles Belden   b: 1855
    3. Anna Martha Belden   b: 1861   d: 1884
  2. Son Fuller   b: abt 1825
  2. Willis Fuller   b: 1828   d: 1900
+ Mary Cole   b: abt 1791   d: bef 1860
  2. Cynthia Fuller   b: 1834
   + James A Elliott   b: 1834
    3. Mary Elliott   b: 1863
    3. John J Elliott   b: 1864
    3. Charles F Elliott   b: 1866
    3. James A Elliott   b: 1867
    3. Harriett Elliott   b: 1873
  2. Maria Fuller   b: 1837
  2. Jacob E Fuller   b: 1838
   + Francis H Greene   b: 1843   d: abt 1871
    3. Mary Fuller   b: 1868
    3. Fanny M Fuller   b: 1870
  2. Harry Fuller   b: 1 Apr 1840   d: 27 Dec 1923
   +Polly Carnahan   b: 27 June 1850   d: 31 Dec 1945
    3. Child Fuller   b: 1870   d: 1870
    3. James Aaron Fuller   b: 1872   d: 1872
    3. Samuel Montgomery Fuller   b: 7 Apr 1875   d: 21 Aug 1970
     + Anna Pearl Woggerman   b : 16 July 1904   d: 21 Aug 1970
      4. Harry Solomon Fuller   b: 26 Aug 1902   d: 17 May 1970
       +Anna Marie Markovic Holms   b: 1904
      4. Sarah Gertrude Fuller   b: 10 Aug 1904
       + Clifford Keck
      4. Kenneth Fuller   b: 1912

3. Lucinda E Fuller   b: 1863   d: 19 Sep 1886
3. James Edward Fuller   b: 21 Dec 1890   d: 8 Nov 1929
  + Lilly Mae Mumea   b: 16 Apr 1891   d: 4 May 1950
      4. Riley Ellis Fuller   b: 21 Feb 1909   d: 25 Nov 1963
      4. Eula Fuller   b: 14 Feb 1912
      4. Velma Fuller   b: 19 Mar 1914
  + Naomi E Wyatt
      4. Charles Leonard Fuller   b: 25 June 1925

# REFERENCES

My deepest appreciation to those who have been so helpful in gathering the information for this document; Carol Thurman, Pat Jimenez, Stefani Ferguson, Donna Wachtel, Janet Beard, Lola Partain, Jennifer Forrest, Belinda Tantalo, and my patient husband, Don Houk, who made the cold and rainy days and nights in northern Ohio a lot of fun.

Selected references (others are included in the document text):

150 Years Along The Riley, 1832-1982
1852 Cuyahoga County Land Ownership Map Index
A Reminiscent History of Brecksville, Centennial
Brecksville Township History
Canals in Paulding County, Ohio, O. Morrow and F. W. Bashore, Historical Atlas of Paulding Co, OH
Cemetery Records
Cuyahoga County Archives
Cuyahoga County Recorder's Office
Death, Administration, Marriage, and Miscellaneous Notices from the Kalida Venture, Putnam Co, OH 1845-1854, Marguerite Crist Calvin
Draft Registration Cards
Early Births of Paulding County, Ray E Keck
Early Marriages of Paulding County, Ray E Keck, 1989
Ethan Allen: His Life and Times, Willard Sterne Randall, W. W. Norton & Company, Inc, New York, NY, 2011
Family documents, photos and records
Findagrave.com
Historical Hand Atlas Paulding County,OH 1882, Paulding County Genealogical Society
History of Columbus Grove http://columbusgroveoh.com
History of Cuyahoga County, OH, Crisfield Johnson, D. W. Ensign & Co, 1879,
History of Geauga and Lake Counties, Sidney Rigdon.com
History of Putnam Co, OH, George D Kinder, B.F. Bowen & Co, Inc, Indianapolis, IN 1915
History of Washington County, New York http://ia700506.us.archive.org
Honor Roll Veterans, Paulding Co, OH 1775-1989, Ray E Keck
Kansas Census records
Oklahoma Land Records
Mary Nussbaum's research notes
Missouri Division of Health – Death Certificates
Mortality Records of Paulding County, OH through 1993, Ray E Keck
Newspaper Notices from Kalida, OH, Putnam Co, 1855-1860, Marguerite Crist Calvin
Newspaper Notices from Kalida, OH, Putnam Co, 1861-1866, Marguerite Crist Calvin
Numerous Land Records
Ohio Obituary Index, 1830s-2009, Rutherford B. Hayes Presidential Center
Once Upon a Sugar Grove, 1864-1964, Columbus Grove, Ohio Centennial

Paulding County Engineer's Office
Paulding County Probate Court Records
Paulding County Recorder's Office
Pension Records
Personal and Pioneer Reminiscences, Part 1, Christopher G. Crary, 1893
Philip Skene of Skenesborough, Doris Begor Morton
Putnam County Births, 1859-1880, M. Utendorf
Putnam County Engineers Office
Putnam County Marriage Records, 1834-1880, M. Utendorf
Putnam County Probate Court Records
Putnam County Recorder's Office
Rootsweb
The Ohio Repository
Townships of Cuyahoga County
U.S. Census Records
Washington County, NY, County Historian
Watt Family Reunion 2000: Histories and Memories, Jennifer Forrest
Whitehall, N.Y. Local History Sketches, Clarence E Holden
Wikipedia
Woods County Oklahoma County History, http://genealogytrails.com

---

POSTNOTE:

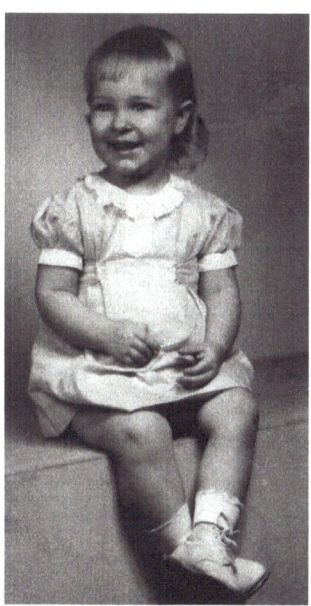

I know that Mary (Johnston) Nussbaum will be pleased to see the compiled history of the Fuller family (as we know it on Oct. 1, 2011) printed. It has also been a blessing to be used by our Lord to facilitate the compilation and publication of the information included. We are not to live in the past, but the present. Yet, our understanding and appreciation of the present cannot be fully understood without a good grounding in the past.

To know our "roots" and to build on them, correcting what needs to be corrected and advancing what is good, is one of our missions on earth. The Fuller family, from the British Empire to the New World, has demonstrated a cohesiveness that should be acknowledged and supported as time goes on. God Bless!

Katherine Louise Whiteside Forrest Houk

www.ingramcontent.com/pod-product-compliance
Lightning Source LLC
Chambersburg PA
CBHW040906020526
44114CB00037B/74